Charles Lutwidge Dodgson could not explain Lewis Carroll and did not try. He *was* Lewis Carroll, and that was enough for him.

About other things, Charles Dodgson-Lewis Carroll was very sure. He was a deacon, a clergyman of the Church of England. He was a mathematician and a college teacher, a don of Christ Church, Oxford. He was a logician who believed with all his mind in sense and a poet who believed with all his heart in nonsense. He lived, and for the most part happily, with them all: mind, heart, sense, and nonsense.

Perhaps it was this that made him different, for Charles Dodgson was odd. He was an eccentric, one who is a little off the center most people think they are on. What center? he would have inquired sharply, and probably he was right. He lived squarely in the center of all that mattered to him.

He loved Christ Church and Oxford, where he lived all of his adult life. He loved small girls like Alice Liddell, but not after they grew up. He had a passion for the church, for clear thought, for the theater, for photography — at which he was expert — but his real passion was for words. He could put them together to build delicate but indestructible fairy tales, to create impossible stories of incredible adventures, to make sense sound like nonsense and nonsense sing like sense, and all of them sound inimitably like Lewis Carroll and nobody else — except, perhaps, Charles Lutwidge Dodgson.

James Playsted Wood

The Snark
Was a Boojum

A Life of Lewis Carroll

WITH DRAWINGS BY DAVID LEVINE

PANTHEON BOOKS

Library of Congress catalog card number: 66-12739

for E.C.W.

I was walking on a hillside, alone, one bright summer day, when suddenly there came into my head one line of verse — one solitary line — "For the Snark *was* a Boojum, you see." I knew not what it meant, then: I know not what it means, now . . .

"Alice on the Stage," *The Theatre*, April 1887

The Snark *Was* a Boojum

One

Charles Lutwidge Dodgson, who was born in Daresbury, Cheshire, in the north of England, January 27, 1832, had only one head. Though he was to be two people, he had only two hands, two feet, and on most days the usual number of noses, fingers, and toes.

If this sounds like nonsense, it should, for Charles Dodgson was also Lewis Carroll, and Lewis Carroll means nonsense. He loved nonsense, created nonsense, talked nonsense when he had the right audience, and wrote the most delightful and sensible nonsense in the English language.

Charles Dodgson knew a man whose feet were so large he had to put on his trousers over his head. He knew that the Snark really is a Boojum, and he knew a queen who sometimes believed as many as six impossible things before breakfast. He knew the Jabberwock only too well, and he warned people solemnly to beware of the frumious Bandersnatch — which is as good a thing to beware of as anything else. Some of this may have been because Dodgson's birthday, so he said, came once every seven years, and always on the fifth Thursday in April.

Some of Dodgson's habits were peculiar. When he was very tired, he went to bed a minute after he got up. When he was even more tired than that, he went to bed a minute *before* he got up. Some of his tastes were unusual too. When he was hungry, he liked a bit of mustard with some beef spread thinly under it, though his favorite dish was salt with some soup spread over it. He loved small girls, and detested small boys. He thought they were a mistake. He could not read too well, which is awkward for a college professor, which he was. Once when a small girl sent him sacks full of love and baskets full of kisses, he thought she had written "a sack full of gloves and a basket full of kittens" and grew very confused.

Lewis Carroll was often as confused as Charles Dodgson was. He was apt to see things backwards or hear them inside out. He associated with clergymen and college teachers, for he was one of each himself, but also with artists, mad hatters, actresses, March hares, and chessmen and sometimes seemed unable to tell any of them apart. Mostly he knew a hawk from a handsaw, but in some moods Charles Dodgson Lewis Carroll, or Lewis Carroll Charles Dodgson, or Charles Lewis Dodgson Carroll — for he was a mathematician and doted on permutations and combinations — thought he could fly down High Street in Oxford on a handsaw and cut down dandelions with a hawk.

He knew Queen Victoria and her consort, Prince Albert,

4

and once he had been the Duke of Wellington, who defeated Napoleon at Waterloo. At least he said he had been, so that is probably just as true as his story about the man who put on his trousers over his head. He also knew a small girl named Alice who followed a rabbit underground into one of the most famous adventures in history, and another Alice who walked right through a looking-glass into a world almost as strange as the one this side of the mirror.

He knew that two and two are four — most of the time — and that you cannot square a circle; though if anyone could, he could, for he could do more things with arithmetic, trigonometry, and calculus than a circus clown can do with a hoop and his oversize shoes. Yet he had trouble with even as simple an act as getting dressed. Sometimes he strove madly to get a right-hand foot into a left-hand shoe.

When Charles Lutwidge Dodgson was born, he already had two sisters, one aged four, the other two. He was the first son among the eleven children, seven of them girls, of the Reverend Charles Dodgson, who had married his first cousin, Frances Jane Lutwidge. Thus the small boy was doubly descended from a great-grandfather who had been a bishop of the Church of England and a reputed humorist as well as a churchman. The clerical tradition was strong in Charles Lutwidge Dodgson's ancestry, and so was the scholarly.

His father, also a wit and humorist, had been a distinguished classical scholar at Christ Church, Oxford, where he took a double first; that is, he took high honors both in Latin and Greek and in mathematics. Mathematics was the favorite study and pastime of the rector of Daresbury. Daresbury itself was a remote and rural place, and the Dodgsons lived in a remote and very rural part of it.

5

The parsonage was on the glebe farm, the fields belonging to the parish church, a mile and a half from the tiny village. The big square brick house stood alone on level ground. It was shaded by tall oaks, for the region was famous for its oaks. The house was so isolated, says Dodgson's nephew and godson Stuart Dodgson Collingwood, that even the passage of a farm cart was an exciting event.

With a large house and a steadily increasing family, Dodgson's gentle mother could have had little time to play with her children. The children's father, grave and deeply religious, though a witty storyteller and always a student, could have had little more. He not only had his parish church services to conduct and his parishioners to guide, but he had also one of the strangest chapels imaginable. A canal flowed slowly through part of Daresbury, and the Reverend Mr. Dodgson thought the bargeman as deserving of the ministrations of the Church of England as their land-locked fellows. He persuaded a titled landowner of the district to have one of the canal barges converted into a chapel. After conducting church services in the village church on Sunday mornings, he conducted another service on shipboard in the evening.

In such an idyllic but removed setting, the Dodgson children had to find or concoct their own amusements, and Charles Dodgson did both for himself and for his sisters. He made pets of toads and snails. He provided earthworms with bits of pipe in an effort to make their warfare more businesslike and effective. Undoubtedly he watched rabbits about their antics, and perhaps one of them was a white rabbit. He saw the small animals of the countryside all about him, and heard the insects whose hum in midsummer was the loudest noise around the parsonage on the glebe farm.

Usually a small sister or two were with him, thus a familiar part of the scene, as familiar as the grass and wildflowers and the birds in the oaks: all the things he was to remember so vividly all his life.

There were always books in the rectory household, too, and probably Charles Dodgson progressed from collections of Mother Goose rhymes — the first, *Mother Goose's Melody*, had been published in London around 1765 — to *Gulliver's Travels* by way of all the many other stories for children that there were in those years. Most of these stories were about fairies, giants, ogres, and strange animals in strange lands. The great Dr. Samuel Johnson, whose authority few disputed, had stated late in the eighteenth century that "babies do not like to hear stories of babies like themselves; that they require to have their imaginations raised by tales of giants and fairies and castles and enchantments." One of Dr. Johnson's close friends was Oliver Goldsmith, who wrote for John Newbery, publisher of *Mother Goose's Melody* and of other children's books. Goldsmith probably wrote *Goody Two-Shoes* himself.

Probably the Dodgson children also read the more factual stories which Maria Edgeworth had written to instill love of justice, truth, and humility in children. They were good stories, and *The Parent's Assistant* was the kind of book apt to be found in the library of a country parsonage.

It was from books like these that small Charles Dodgson learned something of the real world of towns and people, which he seldom saw, but more of the world of fantasy and imagination. To the Dodgson children in their solitude the imaginary world must have seemed the more real of the two. Dodgson mixed them up — he never really learned to separate them — and sometimes confused the religious ideas

7

he got from his father with ideas come from his own acute observations and vivid imaginings. His attempts to arm the ants and earthworms in the garden was one result. Another was that he peeled rushes with the idea that the inner tissue could be given to "the deserving poor," of whom he had heard, and somehow help them out.

Except for infrequent journeys with the family to more populous places, Charles Dodgson spent all of his first eleven years, the formative years of his life, on the glebe lands of Daresbury parish. Except for the occasional companionship of Vere Bayne, son of the headmaster of the grammar school in the larger town of Warrington about seven miles away, he spent all of his time with his parents, his many brothers and sisters, and the household servants. In any large family some of the care of the younger children falls on the older. As the eldest son, Charles probably thought it his duty to help entertain his seven sisters. It was no chore. Quick, clever, with his father's eye for the ridiculous and his witty way with words, he loved it.

The Church of England is a state church. Its "livings" are granted clergymen by the government or by those institutions which, generally from long usage, the government gives the privilege of granting them. The Daresbury living had been in the gift of Christ Church, the Oxford college which the Reverend Mr. Dodgson had attended. In 1843 Sir Robert Peel, another Christ Church man who had taken a double first in classics and mathematics, and had become Conservative Prime Minister of England, bestowed the Crown living of the Yorkshire town of Croft on the rector. A Crown living is a parish post which can be filled at the pleasure of the government itself.

Thus when Charles Dodgson was eleven, the family

moved to a more important parish in a resort town, for Croft, with its medicinal waters, was famed as a spa. Their new home was a two-story brick rectory with a hollow-tile roof and spacious grounds. Near a large hotel, the Croft rectory had its own large and well-tended garden of fruit trees and flowers, for the previous rector had been an enthusiastic gardener.

The Reverend Mr. Dodgson's fortunes continued to rise. He soon moved higher in the Church. He became examining chaplain to the Bishop of Ripon, then was made Archdeacon of Richmond and a canon of Ripon Cathedral. With these posts he retained the living at Croft, and the Croft parsonage remained the Dodgson family home for many years.

This was a more exciting life for the children, and it was made even more exciting when Charles constructed their own private railroad in the beautiful garden. New inventions always fascinated Charles Dodgson, and the railroad was a new and miraculous means of transport in the English countryside of the 1830s and 1840s.

The Dodgson Line consisted of one train. This train, composed of a wheelbarrow, a barrel, and a hand truck, carried passengers from one station to another in the garden. Charles Lutwidge Dodgson, who had built the road, seems also to have acted as president, chief engineer, conductor, and one-boy board of directors. By his edict, all passengers had to purchase tickets before they could board the train. They could purchase refreshments at the stations. He laid down other rules.

Station master must mind his station and supply refreshments: he can put anyone who behaves badly to prison . . . he must ring for the passengers to take their seats, then count 20 slowly, then ring for the train to start. . . . Passengers may not go out on the line on any pretence: parents responsible for their children: may not get in or out of the train when moving: the money is divided equally among all except drivers: the parents take their childrens': any one without money works at one of the stations.

The gay and inventive small boy also felt responsible for the safety, health, and well-being of his passengers, but on his own terms.

All passengers when upset are requested to lie still until picked up — as it is requisite that at least 3 trains should go over them, to entitle them to the attention of the doctor and assistants.

When he was not running his railroad, the vital Charles Dodgson was busy being a magician, a theatrical producer, an actor, and a playwright.

Conservative members of the English clergy frowned on the theater. They were expected to refrain from attending professional performances and to warn their congregations against the evils of theater-going. Either Archdeacon Dodgson did not share this prejudice or he did not include amateur family dramatics in his prohibitions.

Charles Dodgson was always deft with his hands. At eleven, he performed as a magician for his three brothers and seven sisters. Arrayed in a long white robe, probably a surplice of his father's, and a brown wig, he mystified his rapt audience with conjuring and sleight-of-hand. He did more. With the help of the village carpenter and his fam-

10

ily, he carved a troupe of marionettes and built a small theater for them to act in. Not only did he manipulate the complicated strings which controlled the actions of his puppets, but he also dictated their actions by writing the plays for them himself. It wasn't hard for him to do. He could write easily. He could make up a rhyme, particularly a funny rhyme, almost without thinking. If he couldn't find just the word he wanted, he simply made up another and better word of his own.

When he was twelve years old, Charles Dodgson, like most English boys of good family, was sent away to school. The school chosen was Richmond, a preparatory school for boys in Yorkshire not too far from Croft. As a new boy, Dodgson underwent the usual mild hazing. It was not enough to discomfit him. When he wrote home the first time, he had already lost his toothbrush, mislaid his blotting paper, and found he had forgotten to take a shoehorn with him. More important from his viewpoint, he was able to say, "The boys play me no tricks now."

The chief games at Richmond were football, wrestling, leapfrog, and fighting. Dodgson had as little to do with any of these sports as he could. He was never good at games and did not like them. He preferred the gentler pastimes — the railroad, the conjuring, the puppetry for the entertainment of his sisters.

From the first the sharp-witted boy was a good student. By his second year he had written a story, "The Unknown One," for the school magazine. When Charles Dodgson was thirteen, his discerning Richmond headmaster wrote his pupil's parents, and he was unstinting in his praise. He had discovered early what the rest of the world was not to know for some time. Charles Lutwidge Dodgson, he wrote, was gentle and cheerful. He had a love of precise argument, an unusually clear mind that made him capable of reasoning far beyond his years. He had just passed an examination in mathematics with very high marks.

One other thing the headmaster noted with some surprise. When translating or composing Latin verse, Charles did not always abide by the ordinary rhymes and accepted placing of accents. "He is moreover marvellously ingenious in replacing the ordinary inflexions of nouns and verbs . . . by more exact analogies, or convenient forms of his own devising." Wisely, the headmaster warned the parents against letting their son know of his marked superiority over other boys of his age, but he was positive in his own estimate: "I do not hesitate to express my opinion that he possesses, along with other and excellent natural endowments, a very uncommon share of genius."

Charles Dodgson was happy at Richmond, but the boy with "the very uncommon share of genius" was very unhappy at Rugby when he left preparatory school for public school.

With Eton, Harrow, and Winchester, Rugby is one of England's famed public schools. Founded by Laurence Sheriff in 1567, it is distinguished for two reasons. Its headmaster from 1827 to 1842 was Dr. Thomas Arnold, a clergyman and educational reformer who was the father of Matthew Arnold. In 1823, when an excited player broke all existing rules and picked up the football and ran with it, Rugby football, of which American football is an offshoot, originated.

The fame of Rugby has been well advertised. One of the best known English boys' books, *Tom Brown's Schooldays* by Thomas Hughes, was published in 1857. That story describes vividly the discomforts and the sadistic cruelties, the fagging, beatings, and roastings which were practiced on small boys by larger boys in Rugby and the other better English public schools. Only the sons of the better-class English families who could afford the fees were sent to schools like Rugby. Once there, they were expected to endure the torments of their fellows and the severe discipline of the masters as best they could and, in a microcosm of the world at large, learn to give as good as they got. Perhaps it was not a bad system for the competitive, the dull and unimaginative. It was generally not a pleasant experience for the more sensitive and thinner-skinned.

When he became Rugby's headmaster, Dr. Arnold had stated his three aims in what seemed to him the order of their importance: "What we must look for here is, first, religious and moral principles: secondly, gentlemanly conduct: thirdly, intellectual ability." Under Arnold many of the worst Rugby abuses were eradicated. Flogging, fagging, the prefect system of student monitors and its attendant evils survived, but Arnold infused the school with a bright new spirit and a new pride through his sermons and his personal influence.

Dr. Archibald Tait, who later became ecclesiastical head of the Church of England as Archbishop of Canterbury, had succeeded Arnold as headmaster at Rugby. This could have made little difference to Charles Dodgson when he was a new boy. If he was aware of Dr. Arnold's reforms at all, it must have been to wonder how conditions could possibly have been more unpleasant before.

Football and cricket were the great games at Rugby, where, as in the other public schools, a fetish is made of sports. As far as he could, Dodgson ignored them. He tried to ignore as much as possible of the rest of Rugby life. The school was always cold. It was colder at night. To keep warm, older and larger boys in the dormitories ripped the blankets off the beds of helpless smaller boys, who were left to shiver through the night while they waited for the cheerless dawn, followed inevitably by another freezing night. Years later when he was inspecting another public school in which the boys had separate rooms, Charles Dodgson said he could have endured Rugby better if it had not been for the nights in the open dormitory.

At home he was the bright and handsome eldest son. He held the center of the stage. His performances were applauded, and he was admired. At Rugby no one cared that he was clever at parlor games and a wit in the family circle. Rugby stalwarts had only contempt for that kind of thing. One was not supposed to admit that he had sisters, certainly not seven of them.

Dodgson counted the days until vacations, greeted them with relief, and felt exultantly free, happy, and safe at home. Some of his relief and exuberance, as well as his increasing skill as a writer and his sharp sense of the comic, spilled over into the home magazines which he wrote and edited when he was from thirteen to eighteen years old.

Home magazines were not as uncommon a diversion in large but literate Victorian families as they are today. They were an accepted form of entertainment where there were children bright and clever enough to create and enjoy them. The first of these Croft rectory magazines was *Useful and Instructive Poetry*, which lasted for six months in 1845. Then, in 1849 or 1850, came *The Rectory Umbrella*. Stuart Collingwood, Dodgson's first biographer, quotes copiously from pieces which Charles Dodgson wrote and illustrated

— for he was early able to sketch with his pen and pencil as well as to write with them. One of these was a parody of Macaulay's *Lays of Ancient Rome*. Dodgson, with his quick ear, was an instinctive mimic. He supplied comic footnotes and telling cartoons for his ridiculous parody.

At home with his brothers and sisters, Dodgson was at ease. No one noticed the hesitation in his speech, and the family disability — all but four of the eleven Dodgson children stammered to a greater or less degree — disappeared altogether when he was talking with small children. The stammering, which grew worse when he was ill at ease, was undoubtedly mocked and derided at Rugby. At home it went unnoticed. At Rugby, too, Dodgson suffered a worsening of another lifelong minor disability. An attack of the mumps about 1850, when he was seventeen or eighteen, increased the deafness in one ear which had been caused originally by an infantile fever.

Whatever its pain and assorted discomforts, Dodgson's life at Rugby was a success in the way in which he preferred to succeed. Once more he proved himself a brilliant student. His originality in scanning earned him many an imposition — task of copying out lines of Latin over and over — but Charles Dodgson won and took home prize after prize for excellence in his studies. He made few friends at school. At least one and probably more of his fellows considered him a "muff," or milksop, for one of them wrote "is a muff" after Dodgson's signature in a schoolbook, but the boy who knew himself the intellectual superior of most of them had his revenge. Once more, the masters were high in their praises. The mathematics master wrote Archdeacon Dodgson that he had not had a more promising pupil of his son's age since he came to Rugby.

Usually those with literary gifts are poor at mathematics. Charles Dodgson was an exception. His father was a good mathematician. All of the Dodgson children had an aptitude for mathematics. If, as someone has said, mathematicians are born, not made, they were all born mathematicians, and Charles Dodgson started out with a dual talent.

When this unusual pupil finished his public-school year, Dr. Tait wrote the Archdeacon extolling his son's character and accomplishments. He considered Charles Dodgson's abilities outstanding, and mentioned not only his abilities in mathematics but also what he recognized as Dodgson's gift for religious studies. Writing, mathematics, religion gave the boy not a dual but a triple talent.

Two

The Dodgsons must all have enjoyed the eldest son's enviable Rugby record and the praise he received from stern critics. Probably Charles enjoyed it too, but he had other feelings. In later years he wrote, "I cannot say that I look back upon my life in a Public School with any sensations of pleasure, or that any earthly considerations would induce me to go through my three years again."

He was free of it now, and the long summer and autumn of 1850 were pleasant for Charles Lutwidge Dodgson. A schoolboy no longer, he had matriculated — enrolled — at Christ Church, Oxford, his father's college in his father's university. His mother and father were proud of their eldest son, who had already proved his prowess as a scholar and might well duplicate his father's academic accomplishments. His brothers and sisters looked at him with awe and envy, for this would be his entrance into the adult world and into the university world at its finest.

Oxford and Cambridge were the oldest as for six hundred years they had been the only English universities. Merton, founded in 1264, is usually considered the oldest of the Oxford colleges, but Christ Church is the largest, wealthiest, and with Balliol and Magdalen, one of the proudest of them all.

In the mid-nineteenth century there were twenty-odd colleges and halls composing the University of Oxford. Today there are thirty-six, five of them for women. It is in their colleges that undergraduates live, eat, study, and disport themselves. They read in preparation for examinations, conducted by the university, which determine whether or not they receive their degrees and what kind of degrees they receive, merely pass degrees or degrees with honors. These colleges grew originally out of medieval hostels, houses which groups of students hired for themselves and where they lived and studied under the guidance of a master, or teacher. Though he may attend lectures conducted by the university and those held in other colleges, it is in his own college that an Oxford undergraduate reports to his don, or tutor, on the reading or other studies assigned him, usually reading papers he has written to the don in his rooms for his comment and criticism.

There are no discussion classes, no tests, no quizzes. No attendance is taken at lectures. Failure or success depends wholly on the university examinations which the undergraduate must take at the end of his period of residence, which usually is three years. Basically, the function of the college is to prepare its members for these examinations.

In Charles Dodgson's undergraduate days, Oxford was not, as it is now, largely an industrial city, seat of one of the largest automotive plants in England. It was a country town some sixty miles northwest of London, which even then was only about an hour and a quarter away by train. In 1850 it was just the seat of Oxford University, whose ancient halls and gray stone towers dominated the town; and the town fell directly away into the farms, fields, and meadows of a gentle countryside.

The actual name of Christ Church — known as "C.C.C." for Christ Church College but to its own men always as "The House" — is The Dean and Chapter of the Cathedral of Christ in Oxford of the Foundation of King Henry the Eighth. Even that resounding title is somewhat misleading. In 1524 Cardinal Wolsey founded Cardinal College on the site of an eighth-century nunnery in Oxford. He planned it as physically the largest of the Oxford colleges and as a place of real scholarship. Its great hall with its famous kitchen was completed in 1529.

Cardinal Wolsey was deposed in 1529, and his college was suppressed. For several years there were only its buildings. King Henry VIII reinstituted Cardinal as Christ Church under the government of the dean and canons of Oxford Cathedral, the smallest cathedral in England, which is also the chapel of Christ Church College.

Thus, where others of the Oxford colleges are headed by a master, a principal, a president, Christ Church, unique in its founding, is headed by a dean. At the original foundation there were a dean, eight canons, and one hundred students. Christ Church is still headed by a dean, with six canons and about thirty-five students to assist him. A student in Christ Chuch corresponds to a Fellow in the other

19

Oxford colleges. He is a member, usually a teaching member, of the college faculty; a tutor, a don.

Like most of the other colleges in Oxford, Christ Church is made up of several quadrangles: Peckwater, Canterbury, the Great Quadrangle or Tom Quad, which is the largest college quadrangle in Oxford. At the entrance to Tom Quad stands Tom Tower, within it the seven-ton Great Tom bell. Every night at 9:05 it strikes one hundred and one times for the number of students plus one which Christ Church had originally. Tom has been doing this since 1684. This is Oxford's curfew, a warning to undergraduates that they must be in their colleges. Five minutes later all college gates in Oxford are closed.

Wolsey's Great Hall with its fan-vaulted entrance stands in the southeast corner of Christ Church. The Hall, hung with oil paintings of men eminent in the history of the college, is one hundred and fifteen feet long, forty feet wide, and fifty feet from floor to carved oak ceiling. It is here that the undergraduates, with the dons at the head table, dine every evening. They usually breakfast and lunch in their own rooms or in those of friends.

Cambridge has a long literary tradition, numbering Milton, Thomas Gray, Wordsworth, and many others among its men, but Oxford has always been considered the home of English letters. Joseph Addison, the essayist, was at Magdalen; Jeremy Bentham, the political economist, and the essayist and critic Walter Pater were at Queen's. Shelley was expelled from University College, and the great historian Edward Gibbon from Magdalen. Sir Walter Raleigh managed to stay in Oriel, as did Thomas Hughes, who went on from Rugby to write his lesser-known *Tom Brown at Oxford* and to become a judge and social reformer.

20

Thomas Arnold was at Corpus Christi; Thomas De-Quincey, famous for his *Confessions of an English Opium-Eater*, at Worcester; the poet Walter Savage Landor, at Trinity; the essayist and wit Sydney Smith, at New. Balliol, founded in the thirteenth century and thus nearly three hundred years older than Christ Church, had the famous diarist John Evelyn; the economist Adam Smith; Cardinal Henry Edward Manning, great preacher and religious controversialist; the poets Matthew Arnold, Arthur Hugh Clough, and Robert Southey; and the classical scholar Benjamin Jowett. Jowett, a controversial academic figure in Dodgson's time, became the head of his college and complacent hero of a quatrain which, with minor variations, is often repeated.

> Here I stand. My name is Jowett.
> All there is to know, I know it.
> What I don't know isn't knowledge,
> For I am the Master of Balliol College.

When Charles Lutwidge Dodgson took up residence in Peckwater Quad, January 24, 1851, Christ Church stood second to none in the accomplishments of its graduates in letters, statesmanship, and the Church. The essayist Richard Steele had been at Christ Church before he moved over to Merton. Robert Burton, who wrote *The Anatomy of Melancholy*; the philosopher John Locke; the playwright Thomas Otway; John Wesley, the founder of Methodism; the statesman William Ewart Gladstone; the critic and social theorist John Ruskin; and Dr. Edward Pusey were all Christ Church. There would be one more worthy to join this company: Lewis Carroll.

21

Often where a man goes to college or what university he attends is of small importance to him or to anyone else. For all the effect it has upon him or upon the institution, he might as well have gone elsewhere or to no college at all; and the usual effect upon the world at large is nil. Christ Church and Oxford became part of Charles Lutwidge Dodgson, and he became part of them. Oxford, C.C.C., and Lewis Carroll and *Alice in Wonderland* are indissoluble.

The bells and towers of Oxford, The Parks, the Christ Church Meadows opening down to the Isis, which is what that stretch of the Thames River is called, must have been much the same a century and more ago as they are now. Though they wore different clothes and spoke a different slang, the undergraduates could not have been too different either. Some studied and studied hard. Others studied as little as they could. Organized religion was more in evidence and its official observance more marked. There was less science, social science, and pseudo-science. Scholarship was narrower, and general interest was less international than is fashionable now; but life was leisurely in Oxford then, and it still is.

The Oxford academic year is divided into three terms with generous lapses between. It is eight weeks in residence (the Hilary term) followed by six weeks of vacation; a second eight weeks (the Michaelmas) followed by another six-week vacation; a third eight weeks (the Trinity) followed by the long vacation of sixteen weeks. During the long vacation, undergraduates are expected to do assigned reading and sometimes do. The Oxford undergraduate is in attendance for twenty-four weeks, absent for twenty-eight weeks of the year. The usual three years' residence leading to an Oxford Bachelor of Arts degree is actually a residence of less than a year and a half.

During this time it is possible to do very little work and still pass. Many have done it, and many were doing it intently when Charles Dodgson was an Oxford undergraduate.

One of the comic classics of the mid-nineteenth-century in England was *The Adventures of Mr. Verdant Green,* with a profusion of pen-and-ink cartoons by its author, "Cuthbert Bede, B.A." Bede was really the Reverend Edward Bradley, an Anglican rector who was also an illustrator for *Punch.* It recounts with gusto the indignities suffered by the countrified and bespectacled Verdant Green when he entered Brazenface (Brasenose College) and donned his undergraduate's gown. Chaffed and unmercifully befooled by his hearty fellows, he became an inept member of the university's sporting set and with his friends Bouncer and Larkyn progressed awkwardly but happily through a three-year round of delectable diversions. Supper parties, drinking parties, running up debts with the local tradesmen, boxing matches, town-and-gown riots, an occasional brush with tutors, proctors, and a book or two, then some rather cursory examinations, were the basis of his curriculum.

Mr. Green emerged gloriously able to perpetrate the same tricks on unsuspecting freshmen that had been played on him. He was able to sport forever thereafter all the knowingness he had acquired and an Oxford degree with all the rights and privileges pertaining thereto. Verdant was as happily innocent when he left Oxford as when he entered it, and just as happy as if he had partaken of the intellectual delights which were there but which no one had thought to point out to him.

Probably no one thought to point out to Charles Dodgson that the college life which Verdant Green, Larkyn, and Bouncer celebrated was there. Undoubtedly he knew of the fox-hunting proclivities and sporting life of the wealthy and often grandly titled undergraduates, which enabled them to endure the boredom of Oxford residence, but this was a world he did not know and did not want.

In only one of the activities in which Verdant Green participated would he have been interested. At a Christmas party during vacation Mr. Green had been dancing polka after polka with Miss Patty Honeywood and dancing as often as possible beneath the mistletoe, but Miss Honeywood had a rival, and her rival a magic box.

> It was perhaps ungrateful in our hero to prefer Miss Patty Honeywood to Miss Fanny Bouncer ... Especially ... as there was nothing to be objected to in Miss Bouncer, saving the fact that some might have affirmed she was a trifle too much inclined to *embonpoint*, and was indeed a bouncer in person as well as in name. Especially, too, as Miss Fanny, being mistress of the usual young-lady accomplishments, was a clever proficient in the fascinating art of photography, and had brought her camera and her chemicals, and had not only calotyped Mr. Verdant Green, but had made no end of duplicates of him, in a manner that was suggestive of the deepest admiration and affection.

Bede's accompanying cartoon shows the buxom Miss Bouncer with her head covered by a cloth viewing her seated subject through the lens of a box camera on a stout tripod. The newly invented photography was all the rage as a parlor entertainment in the early 1850s. In *The Adventures of Mr. Verdant Green* it even becomes the subject of an elaborate charade. Charles Dodgson would have liked that, for charades were a favorite amusement in the Croft rectory, and he would have guessed the answer immediately. He was to become a famed photographer.

Charles Dodgson entered Christ Church with the ability and the determination to excel in the academic world. Undoubtedly he hoped to duplicate his father's feats, and the family hoped that he would follow his father's profession and become the gifted parish priest in a Christ Church living. Well equipped and well connected, he might become an archdeacon, a canon, even a bishop.

His father's friends in Oxford, who knew of his coming, were on the lookout for him, and one of the canons wrote warmly to the Archdeacon welcoming his son to The House. When the young and almost girlishly good-looking freshman arrived, he was unable to obtain rooms in the college. One of the tutors, a clergyman as most were, generously lent him one of his own rooms until Dodgson was able to obtain lodgings in Peckwater Quad. He started his college career under the most favorable auspices, for Dr. Edward Bouverie Pusey, Regius Professor of Hebrew and a canon of Christ Church, was one of his father's close friends.

The beginning was propitious, but almost immediately there was tragedy that may well have been one of the determining influences in Charles Dodgson's life. He had been in Christ Church for just two days when, the day before his nineteenth birthday, his mother died and he was hastily summoned home to Croft for her funeral. The sudden loss shocked Dodgson. It has been conjectured, reasonably, that it was a blow from which he never fully recovered.

Not too much is known of the four years which Dodgson spent in Christ Church as an undergraduate. He had not yet begun to keep his diary. About all we know of his social activities is that he dined in hall with his own mess at one of the long tables. The food may have been substantial, but it was served on crude pewter plates, and each man hacked what he wanted off the joint of meat as it was passed around. Another member of this mess was Theophilus Carter. Carter later had a furniture shop on the High, but he lives in history because the high hat he always wore and some of his odd notions gave Dodgson an idea.

What is known about Dodgson's undergraduate years is the succession of academic honors that came to the brilliant and hard-working student.

On November 1, 1851, he was awarded a Boulter scholarship. In 1852 he took his Mods — Moderations, or the "Little-Go," are the examinations at the end of the undergraduate's residence in Oxford — and emerged with First Class Honors in mathematics and a Second Class in classical studies. On Christmas Eve of this same year, 1852, on the recommendation of Dr. Pusey, he was made a student of Christ Church.

The nomination was made without favor or influence. As Dr. Pusey was careful to write Archdeacon Dodgson, his son was the choice of the college. According to form, the censor had submitted five names to the dean for consideration, but the college officials had made it plain that they felt Charles Lutwidge Dodgson best qualified for the desirable post. Not in twenty years, said Dr. Pusey, had he given a studentship to any friend on the basis of friendship. He had passed over the sons of men to whom he was indebted. It had given him very great pleasure, and he underlined the "very great," to nominate Charles Lutwidge Dodgson solely on merit.

This was the most important event in the life of Charles

26

Dodgson to this time. It was the event that determined his professional career. Provided he remained unmarried and proceeded to take priest's orders in the Church of England, a man could hold his Christ Church studentship for life.

Now a member of the college tutorial staff, Dodgson took Third Class Honors in Greats — that is, in the humanities — in 1854. This was not his subject, for he disliked both history and philosophy. In the final written and oral examinations in October 1854, he headed the list of five men who took First Class Honors in mathematics.

It was an outstanding achievement. Congratulations poured in on the young student. He won prize after prize. He was in line for both a senior scholarship and a lectureship. The conventional modesty with which he wrote his father hardly hides his jubilation; and the letter contains a comparison which sounds less like the student who had spent weeks of thirteen-hour days preparing for his examinations than like the Lewis Carroll who had not yet come back into the open: "I am getting quite tired of being congratulated on various subjects: there seems to be no end of it. If I had shot the Dean I could hardly have had more said about it."

There were times a few years later when Dodgson would have liked to shoot the dean or preferably his wife and possibly both, but this was not done in Christ Church, and he did not do it.

Dodgson took his Bachelor of Arts Degree December 18, 1854. Early in 1855, on the appointment of a new dean, he was made a Master of the House, that is, a Master of Arts within the precincts of Christ Church. He became a Master of Arts of Oxford University in 1857, after fulfilling the residence requirements for that degree.

When he was first appointed student, Dodgson's college duties were not defined. He merely took attendance at compulsory morning chapel, and in 1855 tutored private pupils, but he began tutoring Christ Church undergraduates in a regular program during the last terms of the year. Soon he was teaching mathematics regularly, on some days for as long as seven hours.

Soon after he began these academic duties, Dodgson wrote a sister and his much younger brother, Edwin, a thank-you letter in which he told them just how he went about his teaching. His methods were his own.

> My dear Henrietta,
> My dear Edwin,
>   I am very much obliged by your nice little gift — it was much better than a cane would have been — I have got it on my watch-chain, but the Dean has not yet remarked it.
>   My one pupil has begun his work with me, and I will give you a description how the lecture is conducted. It is the most important point, you know, that the tutor should be *dignified* and at a distance from the pupil, and that the pupil should be as much as possible *degraded*.
>   Otherwise, you know, they are not humble enough.
>   So I sit at the further end of the room; outside the door (*which is shut*) sits the scout [college servant]; outside the outer door (*also shut*) sits the sub-scout; half-way downstairs sits the sub-sub-scout; and down in the yard sits the *pupil*.
>   The questions are shouted from one to the other, and the answers come back in the same way — it is rather confusing till you are well used to it. The lecture goes on something like this: —

Tutor. What is twice three?
Scout. What's a rice-tree?
Sub-Scout. When is ice free?
Sub-sub-scout. What's a nice fee?
Pupil (timidly). Half a guinea!
Sub-sub-scout. Can't forge any!
Sub-Scout. Ho for Jinny!
Scout. Don't be a ninny! . . .

Not all that Dodgson gleefully reported to his small sister and brother was true. Usually he admitted the pupil to his room, though as often the pupil was sorry he got inside. The dialogue Dodgson reported probably never took place, even in Oxford, but some of what he wrote as nonsense, Dodgson meant.

He really believed that the don should be dignified and the undergraduate degraded into proper humility. He did not like his pupils, and usually they did not like him. Charles Dodgson reserved his humor for his family and associates. He had none for his undergraduates. He never as much as smiled when he spoke to them. His manner was formal and chilly. He never betrayed the slightest interest in his pupils or in their concerns. They found him dry and dull. Some thought him so bad that they petitioned to be transferred to another don.

Perhaps the undergraduates reminded the tutor of the boys at Rugby, where he had had to repress his natural gifts for words and parody. There seems to have been almost contempt in Dodgson's attitude toward the young men of Christ Church who came to him for instruction in mathematics. He let them see none of his wit and fancy or any of the elation he felt.

He had made his mark. He was established in The House.

He was financially independent with an income from his studentship and other duties — he was appointed Sub-librarian in February 1855 — of more than three hundred pounds a year, better than $1,500 at the time. This was a sizable income for a twenty-three-year-old unmarried don in 1855.

In later years Charles Dodgson derided the system under which a young man could achieve a permanent position on the basis of competitive examinations taken after three or four years of university instruction and cramming, then rest forever on his laurels. He had no objections to the system now. Academically he had proved his worth, and he would not have to prove it again. He was free of the fear of examinations, free of the discipline he had exacted of himself, free to think, write, go to the theater, mingle in society as he wished — and he took full advantage of the new-found freedom he had earned.

As a boy he had built his own theater, created his own puppets, written his own plays. Now, despite official Church disapproval of such indulgence, he went to every theatrical performance in Oxford and to every dramatic reading. He went as often as he could to London to gorge himself on everything the theaters there were offering. At Croft during the frequent Oxford vacations, he disported himself and diverted his family with still another magazine, *Misch-Masch*. This was different from the earlier rectory periodicals. It contained clippings of humorous verse and prose that he was already contributing to London papers, and other pieces that he wrote and stored there for possible future use.

The wealthy *Illustrated News* in London had started *The Comic Times* under the editorship of Edmund Yates. Frank Smedley, a distant connection of the Dodgsons, did some work for it. Smedley asked him for contributions, and

Charles Lutwidge Dodgson began to write for publication. When *The Comic Times* changed owners, its original staff started a new magazine, *The Train*, and Dodgson published a number of poems in it in 1856.

One poem he did not send to Yates. He merely entered it in *Misch-Masch*, either during the long vacation or at Christmas 1855. According to Collingwood, he had first composed it for a word game when he was visiting some cousins named Wilcox at Whitburn near Sutherland. Dodgson, who lettered it in ancient script and backward, called it a "Stanza of Anglo-Saxon Poetry."

No one knew what it meant at the time. Most were not even sure how to pronounce some of the words. Perhaps it was Charles Lutwidge Dodgson's comment on life and the world and his part in it to this time. Perhaps he didn't know what it meant either until Humpty Dumpty explained it to Alice sixteen years later. Even Humpty Dumpty, for he was rather cocksure and conceited, could have been wrong. Whatever it means or doesn't mean, the eerie and musical stanza, which rings true and sounds as if it is true — that is the awful thing about it — has haunted people for a long time.

> 'Twas brillig, and the slithy toves
>   Did gyre and gimble in the wabe;
> All mimsy were the borogoves,
>   And the mome raths outgrabe.

The Charles Lutwidge Dodgson who wrote these lines was energetic, eager, and curious. Literally let out of school, he was a hard-working tutor, but he was also a pleasure-loving and pleasure-seeking young man constantly on the lookout for new diversions and entertainment.

He dined out. He lunched out. He went to plays, exhibitions, and lectures. He visited friends. He went on a tour of Wordsworth's Lake District in the north of England. He had thrilled to the Great Exhibition in London which six million people attended in 1851. He went into raptures over Charles Kean as Cardinal Wolsey in *Henry VIII* and Kean's wife as Queen Catherine — "the greatest theatrical treat I ever had or ever expect to have. . . . never shall I forget that wonderful evening, that exquisite vision."

He heard Jenny Lind sing in Handel's *Messiah*. He wrote a poem on Florence Nightingale for *The Train*. When his brothers Wilfred and Skeffington entered Christ Church as undergraduates, he showed them about the college and university as one who had earned the right. All his life he delighted in acting as guide to Oxford, learning dates and anecdotes with the care that marked everything he attempted and spouting them with enthusiasm. At the Princess's Theatre in London, where he had first seen the Keans, he first saw Ellen Terry, aged eight, as Mamillius in *A Winter's Tale* and was enraptured anew.

As he would for all the rest of his life, Dodgson devoured the theater. To him London meant the theater. "Went up to town for a change" occurs and recurs so often in his diary that he might as well have said sometimes that he "went down to Oxford for a change."

Comedies, operas, operettas, farces, one-act plays, tragedies; when it was not these it was musicals, pantomimes, music-hall turns. In Oxford or at Croft it was charades and

To Dodgson, London meant the theater.

amateur theatricals. Dodgson loved plays and play-acting. More the pleasure-seeking sybarite than the solitary ascetic he has often been pictured, he was almost feverish in his search for entertainment in these years. When there were not enough plays to sate his appetite, Dodgson went to the courts to witness the trials of petty criminals. He saw the trials as drama and seems peculiarly unfeeling about the fortunes of those involved.

With his brothers and other friends, Dodgson disported himself on the river Isis or went to the college boat races. These are bump races, in which the crew of one college tries to bump the shell of another out of position and thus move ahead in the rating. It was poor steering that, disappointed, Dodgson blamed for the bad showing of The House in one race week.

He went through a glassworks. He went to fireworks displays. He went to see a ship launched. Dodgson was an insistent sightseer. If there was anything to be looked at anywhere, he went and looked at it and usually was impressed with something about it. He had his father's dignity of mien and carriage, but it seemed to disguise a restlessness in the younger Dodgson that he could not appease.

Though he may never have fully recovered from its effects, he was over the first shock of his mother's death. The dismal experiences at Rugby were receding into the past. The grind of striving for university honors was over. He was his own man now with his own money in his own pockets. He had lost time to make up for and things to do, all kinds of things.

The year 1856 was a packed and busy year for Charles Dodgson, who was now very much the academic man and the socially acceptable young man in black frock coat, white linen, and the gray cloth gloves — mark of the Victorian gentleman — which he wore winter and summer. Early in the year he received his formal appointment as mathematical lecturer in Christ Church. He gave his first two lectures in the lecture room of the college on January 28. One lecture was on Euclidean geometry to nine undergraduates; the other, on algebra to eleven.

This same month he wrote his Uncle Skeffington in London and asked him to get him a camera and photographic apparatus. He had become interested in photography through watching his uncle take pictures in September of the previous year, and he wanted to try the new art. He wanted, as he said, some other occupation in Oxford besides merely reading and writing; though he was doing enough of both in addition to his teaching to keep an ordinary young man more than busy.

The next month Dodgson sent *The Train* a poem titled "Solitude," which he had written three years before. Edmund Yates accepted it, but asked that he sign it with a pen name and asked for one. Dodgson proposed several, all of them variations on his real name. The one which Yates selected was "Lewis Carroll" — Lewis for Ludovicus, or Lutwidge, and Carroll for Carolus, or Charles. The poem was published in the March 1856 issue of the magazine. It was a serious, not a comic, poem, conventional and derivative. It was undistinguished for either thought or music, but its last stanza was prophetic.

> I'd give all wealth that years have piled,
>   The slow result of life's decay,
> To be once more a little child
>   For one bright summer-day.

35

Lewis Carroll was already looking back nostalgically to his childhood.

Early in March, Dodgson made friends with a small boy whom he had first met down by the boats on the Isis at the bottom of Christ Church Meadows. The boy was Harry Liddell, "certainly the handsomest boy I ever saw."

Dodgson seldom bothered with small boys, then or later. It was always to small girls, and then only if they were physically attractive, that he was drawn. Harry was the oldest child and at that time the only son of Dean and Mrs. Henry George Liddell. Their oldest children when they first came to Oxford were three little girls: Lorina, Alice, and Edith. Alice at that time was just three years old.

Liddell, who had been chaplain to Prince Albert, German-born consort of Queen Victoria, had become headmaster of the Westminster School. He had been appointed Dean of Christ Church upon the death of Dean Gaisford. Dean Liddell had been a brilliant undergraduate at Christ Church from 1830 to 1833. Later with Robert Scott, already appointed Master of Balliol, he had written a famous Greek-English lexicon.

Dodgson had profited immediately by Dean Liddell's appointment, being made a Master of the House in honor of the event, but the college had not been too happy about Liddell's appointment. Handsome, stern, dictatorial, quickly aggressive in his handling of Christ Church matters, Liddell was not a warm or friendly man. His wife, as handsome as he, was equally formidable. Both were extremely conscious of their enviable position as the first family of Christ Church.

With their children it was different. In an entirely male and largely monastic institution, attractive children were rare, and Dodgson, who had grown up with a bevy of small sisters, missed the companionship of little girls. The acquaintanceship began with Harry, but soon he was on friendly and intimate footing with all the Liddell children. The instrument was his camera.

For whatever reason, his Uncle Skeffington did not fulfill Dodgson's request to get him a camera. On March 17, 1856, Dodgson met a fellow don named Southey, who was already an amateur enthusiast, in London. Together they went to a camera maker, Ottewill in Charlotte Street, Caledonian Road, where Dodgson bought a camera, lens, and all the rest of the elaborate equipment needed in those early days of wet-plate photography.

With Southey for instructor, Dodgson started out to practice. Inevitably, his first attempts were failures. Small and easily portable cameras with dry spool or pack film had not yet been developed. Taking a picture involved much more than merely snapping a button or adjusting for focus, exposure time, and lens opening. The photographer had to lug about a large camera, a heavy tripod, and a darkroom tent. He had to keep his plates wet with collodion and have with him a set of all the necessary chemicals to prepare, develop, and fix his plates. He had to be at the same time stevedore, artist, scientist, and engineer. Dodgson, with his vivid imagination, his mathematician's love of precision, and his manual dexterity, delighted in being them all.

Not until early June did he make his first successful pictures. By this time photography had already become for him much more than merely something to do besides reading and writing. It fascinated him. He read about it, wrote about it, spent blissful hours in the darkroom with his chemicals, and happy painstaking hours arranging both his paraphernalia and his subjects. The subjects had to pose

37

anywhere from five seconds to two minutes, depending on the light.

One of Dodgson's first attempts with Southey was a picture of Christ Church Cathedral from the deanery gardens. The cathedral did not interest him much. Taking pictures of the Liddell children did. On June 26, 1856, he spent the whole morning at the deanery photographing them.

The Liddell children were the first portrait subjects of Lewis Carroll, described by Helmut Gernsheim as one of the most distinguished amateur portraitists of the mid-Victorian era and "the most outstanding photographer of children in the nineteenth century."

That afternoon, Dodgson with his friend the Reverend Henry Parry Liddon, at that time a member of Christ Church, went to a horticultural show in the gardens of Worcester College. After that, he and another friend rowed down the Isis in a gig, or light rowboat. Harry Liddell acted as stroke of the crew and steered the boat back. Dodgson loved the Isis, but photography was a passion. He determined to tour the Holy Lands with his camera, but right then his chief studio was the deanery, and his chief subjects were the Liddell children.

He took pictures of them at home again on the morning of November 14, 1856, and, at Harry's request, returned in the afternoon to take more pictures of him and of Ina. When Dodgson arrived at the deanery, he was told that Mrs. Liddell had issued orders that no more pictures were to be taken until the family could pose as a group.

Dodgson was affronted and hurt. "This may be meant as a hint," he wrote in his diary that night, "that I have intruded on the premises long enough: I am quite of the same opinion myself, and, partly for this reason, partly because

I cannot afford to waste any more time on portraits at such a bad season of the year, I have resolved not to go back again for the present, nor at all without invitation, except just to pack up the things and bring them back."

Wellborn and well connected, accomplished as he knew himself to be, Dodgson seemed not to recognize a social distinction of which Mrs. Liddell was very conscious. Henry Liddell was the distinguished dean of proud Christ Church, and she was his distinguished wife. They had academic ambitions which in time would make Dean Liddell a Professor of Moral Philosophy and then Vice-Chancellor of Oxford, the real head of the entire university, for the chancellorship was an honorary post bestowed on favored public men. Archbishop Laud had been Chancellor of Oxford. So, although Oxford had been Royalist headquarters during the Civil Wars, had Oliver Cromwell.

In Mrs. Liddell's views, Charles Lutwidge Dodgson was a mere don. It was as if in an American college an instructor, or at best an assistant professor, had made himself too much at home in the president's house.

Yet only a few nights later Dodgson was dining again at the deanery and obviously pleased about it.

Dodgson's moods went up and down. He was photographing, preparing his lectures, reading everything in sight: novel after novel, mathematical works, poetry. He was writing serious verse, humorous verse, prose squibs. He was even reading medical books and starting to build what became a very substantial medical library.

It was an incident on a Saturday in March 1856 that led to this new interest. That morning he saw a man taken with an epileptic fit as he was leaving the Anatomical School Quad. Dodgson caught him as he fell, loosened his collar, and dashed water into his face. A man delivering coal rushed into the medical building and brought out a doctor. Later the doctor, Southey, and Dodgson half led, half carried the stricken man to his rooms near Christ Church Meadows and took turns watching over him until a nurse could be found. Dodgson was determined that next time he would be better prepared to meet such an emergency. He went at the new study with his accustomed zeal. It has been said that had he not succeeded so well in other fields, he might well have made an outstanding physician.

Dodgson's life was full, but it was not all cakes and ale, or even the sherry and biscuits which he preferred.

Three

He was unhappy about his teaching. That autumn he examined six or eight undergraduates who were preparing for the Little-Go. Hardly one of them, he thought, was fit to stand for the examination. He felt tired and discouraged.

He worried on still another score, a matter of essential import to him. Part of the obligation entailed by his studentship was that he "proceed to Holy Orders." Dodgson wished to. The Church was his family profession. He was sincerely religious, genuinely pious, but there were hindrances, physical, mental, and emotional.

Part of the solemnity and stiffness he displayed in his lectures sprang from fear. He feared that if he deviated from the set pattern of his talk he might begin to stammer and bring down on himself the ridicule of his pupils.

The same speech handicap would be a severe detriment in reading the lessons in the church service or in preaching.

When he was with children the stammer disappeared. When he was in congenial company telling a joke or an amusing anecdote — and he was famous for them — to his fellows in the Great Hall, he could use his stammer effectively to hold up the point for just that added moment of suspense. In formal discourse, where he was made more than usually nervous by his awareness of an expectant audience, his stammer was always threat enough to make him break into a sweat.

He had no religious doubts. He was as conservative, as unquestioning as his archdeacon father. He did have doubts that he could parry effectively the attacks of unbelievers and argue cogently for Christianity as understood by the Church of England. At least he told himself that he did not feel well enough prepared for such a clerical duty.

To retain his studentship he was obliged to enter the Church, and he still wished to, but there was one delight he could not relinquish, the theater. The footlights, the actors, the action, the sound and color, the whole make-believe world of the theater enthralled him. In the theater he could dwell undisturbed in the world of imagination and let his fancy dance to the music of life. Many of the older clergy, among them the Bishop of Oxford, proscribed the theater for men of the cloth. The theater, they held, was a work of the devil with which a man of God could hold no intercourse. This Dodgson did not believe.

As a clergyman he would command more respect from the undergraduates, and this was always important to Charles Dodgson, but could he be a skillful clergyman and could he forswear the delights of the London stage?

For the time being Dodgson solved his dilemma by avoiding it. He adopted diversionary tactics. He bought a magic lantern, took it home to Croft at Christmas, and staged a two-and-a-half-hour show for children, family, friends, and servants. He loved gadgets that would entertain.

Friendly relations with the deanery were re-established, disestablished, re-established. It went like that. Mrs. Liddell's dislike of Dodgson seemed to become sharper. As an overture, he offered to teach Harry Liddell mathematics. Mrs. Liddell reported the suggestion to her mother. When Dodgson next called at the deanery the children's governess, Miss Prickett, informed him that Mrs. Reeves had written saying she feared this would overwork the child's brain. Dodgson disagreed, but there was nothing he could do about it.

He was pleased the following Sunday when, after he had read the second lesson in the chapel service, Harry ran up to him and exclaimed, "You've got your white gown on, and you *read in the church!*"

Dodgson took Harry to chapel with him May 17, 1857, and after service walked back to the deanery with all the Liddell children. This time he was more than unpleasantly surprised when he got there. He was disconcerted and disturbed. That night he wrote in his diary: "I find to my great surprise that my notice of them [the children] is construed by some men into attentions to the governess, Miss Prickett. I had a long talk with Joyce about it in the evening . . . it would be inconsiderate to the governess to give any further occasion for remarks of the sort. For this reason I shall avoid taking any public notice of the children in future . . ."

Dodgson was taken aback, either by the actual rumor or

by someone's insinuation that such rumor existed or could be caused.

Another consideration under which he held his studentship was that he remain unmarried. Thus there was sound practical reason for his avoiding feminine entanglement. There were deeper nervous and emotional reasons as well. The one element that is conspicuously lacking in Charles Dodgson's social activities as a young man about town — two towns, Oxford and London — is the feminine. There is no hint in his diary, or in what is known of his life, of any emotional involvement with any young woman, not so much as an innocent flirtation.

That Dodgson possessed normal masculine instincts and impulses is apparent, but he was too busy, too intent on his careers as mathematician and writer — and far too prudish. Perhaps through his upbringing in a religious and dominantly female household, perhaps through an overzealous adherence to the Victorian idealization of woman, perhaps through some damage to his psyche in boyhood or youth, he seems to have had a fastidious and almost morbid horror of sex.

Dodgson adored pretty small girls, an adoration that grew almost into an obsession in later life. He liked mature women who through social position, age, or marriage to his friends were safely out of reach and kept nonpredatory by circumstance or convention, but that was all the feminine companionship he allowed himself. The abnegation may well account for some of his incessant busyness, his need to

The Victorian idealization of women

fill every waking hour with work, diversion, even the complicated clerical tasks of recording and filing his papers, correspondence, photographs, and negatives which he set for himself. It may account in part for the straight-backed dignity he seldom let relax. The combination of caution and prudishness with whatever other element of character or temperament there was kept him a celibate bachelor.

The alarm at the deanery rumor passed and with it his resolve not to see the children. The small Liddells, Miss Prickett and all, were soon in his rooms again as often as he could entice them there to pose and photograph them, especially Alice.

To put the children at ease for the ordeal of sitting still before the camera, he entertained them with stories and pictures. They sat each side of him on a big sofa while he told them stories, improvising as he went along, just as he had done for his small sisters years before. He drew pictures to illustrate the stories as he told them. Besides the stories and his pen or pencil pictures, there were toys for them to play with. There might be the promise of tea and little cakes.

When they were amused and happy, he sat the children before his camera, posed them exactly, arranged the background, carefully composed his picture. He took pictures of Alice again and again. One a few years later shows her in rags, hand held out appealingly, as a beggar girl.

He was more than ever at the deanery. Every summer he took the children four or five times for excursions on the Isis. Always he brought a big basket full of cakes and a kettle for boiling water for tea. Sometimes these were day-long excursions with Skeffington or Wilfred to help row. Often, Robinson Duckworth of Trinity College was the

46

other oarsman. A favorite outing was down the river to Nuneham with a big lunch of chicken and salad in one of the picnic shelters that had been built there in the woods. On these occasions Dodgson left his required Oxford subfusc (black or very dark gray clothes) in his rooms with his gray gloves and arrayed himself in white flannels and a hard straw boater hat. As they rowed or floated on the Isis, Dodgson told the children stories, old stories, new stories, stories that he invented as he rowed, and always they demanded more.

The Liddells were not the only children whose pictures he took. In 1857 he photographed a party which included a Mrs. Weld and her little girl, Agnes Grace, whom he took in costume as Little Red Riding Hood. Mrs. Weld was a sister-in-law of Alfred Lord Tennyson, England's popular Poet Laureate. She sent Tennyson a copy of the picture. Tennyson declared it "indeed a gem." A copy of one of Dodgson's photographs of Alice Liddell, Tennyson called the finest photograph of a child he had ever seen.

Great men were always visiting Oxford, and Charles Dodgson, ever impressed by literary, artistic, and political celebrities, usually managed to meet them and, if possible, to photograph them. Tennyson he described as "a strange, shaggy-looking man . . . his hair, moustache and beard looked wild and neglected. . . . His hair is black: I think the eyes too; they are keen and restless — nose aquiline — forehead high and broad — both face and head are fine and manly. His manner was kind and friendly from the first: there is dry lurking humor in his style of talking." Dodgson saw with an artist's sharp eye.

He asked Tennyson what a passage in one of his poems meant. Tennyson answered that it meant anything the words might mean. This was an answer which later Dodgson himself was apt to give when asked what something he had written meant.

This same year Dodgson managed to meet William Makepeace Thackeray, the novelist, who was then at the height of his fame. They breakfasted together at Lincoln College. He wanted to photograph Thackeray, but the novelist could not find time for the eager twenty-five-year-old photographer.

Charles Dodgson has often been pictured as being a shy and gentle recluse. He never was. In after years he was sometimes aloof and abrupt, and with work to be done he insisted on his privacy. He exacted the privileges of fame after it came, but he was never backward about pushing and pushing hard for what he wanted. He was insistent and persistent when he had an objective in view. When he wanted artistic advice, he did not hesitate to approach John Ruskin, then Slade Professor of Art and one of the great of the university. When he wanted help with some medical problem, he consulted Sir James Paget, the famed surgeon.

He was continuing his medical studies. It may have been this but more likely it was his ever-pressing curiosity that took him to St. Bartholomew's Hospital in London, December 19, 1857, to witness the amputation of a man's leg. "I fully expected to turn ill at the sight," he wrote in his diary, ". . . was much surprised to find that I could bear it perfectly well. I doubt if I could have done this had the man been suffering pain all the while, but it was quite evident that he felt nothing." The precise young mathematician who was so gentle with pretty little girls was more interested in his own reactions than in the fate or emotions of the patient. Charles Lutwidge Dodgson was a young man of many contradictions, but he was single-minded in pursuing his ambitions.

He knew that he had been accused of lion-hunting and pushing himself forward, for he defended himself in a letter of April 1859 to a cousin, William Wilcox. He had been to the Isle of Wight, where Tennyson lived, and had made it a point to call at Farringford, the Laureate's home. "W. must have basely misrepresented me if he said that I followed the Laureate down to his retreat, as I went, not knowing he was there, to stay with an old friend at Freshwater. Being there, I had the inalienable right of a free-born Briton to make a morning call, which I did."

Dodgson came on Tennyson, who was very shortsighted, wearing spectacles and a wide-awake and mowing his lawn. After Dodgson reminded him of who he was, the poet showed him about his lawn and gardens and the house. A habitual smoker, he offered his unexpected guest a pipe. Dodgson, who never smoked, refused. He met the Tennyson children, then returned that evening for tea and the next night for dinner.

They looked at the Tennyson's photograph album. Every upper-class Victorian family had at least one album. The proofs of *The Idylls of the King* were lying about, but Tennyson would not allow Dodgson to look at them. He said that after working hard on verse all day he often dreamed poetry at night, but little of what he dreamed made sense when he awoke. "You, I suppose, dream photographs." It was as a photographer, not yet as a writer, that Tennyson and everyone else looked on Lewis Carroll at this time.

Sir John Simon, an old Christ Church man who was a friend of Tennyson's, was there that night. When he left, Simon offered Dodgson a lift back to the hotel in his car-

riage. Before they got in, he asked politely whether Dodgson objected to his smoking a cigar as they rode. "He didn't object to two pipes in that little den upstairs," growled Tennyson, "and *a feebliori* he's no business to object to one cigar in a carriage."

A few years later Dodgson and his sisters compiled and published, with Tennyson's consent, an index to *In Memoriam* and Dodgson did some swapping with Tennyson's small son, Lionel. He visited the Tennysons again during an Easter vacation and got both Lionel and his older brother Hallam to sign their names in his autograph album. The bargain with Lionel was that they should exchange manuscript copies of their verse. Lionel agreed to take some of Dodgson's in return for his, but exacted conditions. Dodgson had to play a game of chess with him. Dodgson did and won. Dodgson also had to let him give him one blow on the head with a mallet. After some persuasion, Lionel relented and let Dodgson go with his head intact.

Dodgson was successful — to a point — with Tennyson but less successful with other photographic prey. If he admired famous men, he worshipped royalty, and he saw his chance when Victoria herself and Prince Albert paid a surprise visit to Oxford and Christ Church. The Queen, Princess Alice, the Prince of Wales, Prince Alfred, and all their suite explored the Great Hall, the cathedral, and the college library. In the evening there was a great entertainment at the deanery with *tableaux vivants* acted out for the royal guests.

Dodgson described Tennyson as "a strange, shaggy-looking man."

51

Earlier in the day Dodgson had got an aide, General Bruce, to promise him an introduction to the Prince Consort. He had asked to photograph Albert and been refused. Now he apologized for having been so importunate. Little Edith Liddell went by. This gave Dodgson an opportunity to ask whether the Prince had seen any of his photographs of children. The Prince admitted that he had and said that he had admired them.

"I then said," Dodgson wrote in his diary, "I hoped, as I had missed the photograph, he would at least give me his autograph in my album, which he promised to do. Thinking I had better bring the talk to an end, I concluded by saying that, if he would like copies of any of my photographs, I should feel honoured by his accepting them, he thanked me for this, and I then drew back, as he did not seem inclined to pursue the conversation."

A cat may look at a king, a subject on which Dodgson was later to expound at some length, but an amateur photographer, even if he is a good one and, surprisingly, a don of Christ Church, may not importune a prince. Dodgson had been royally snubbed, and he knew it.

Four

The question of his entering the Church continued to press, and Dodgson continued to hesitate. He wished but he did not wish to assume the cloth. The dean was a churchman. So was Robinson Duckworth. His friend Henry Liddon of Christ Church was beginning to be well known for his sermons. Dodgson knew that both his family and the college expected him to take Orders. He also knew all his objections, and a pronouncement of Oxford's Bishop Samuel Wilberforce gave him new pause.

Wilberforce said that attending the theater or the opera was an absolute disqualification for Holy Orders.

With some relief, Dodgson found out that the Bishop meant his dictum to apply only to the parish clergy and not to Oxford dons. Still he was not satisfied. He discussed the subject of his entering the Church with his father's friend Dr. Pusey, then with his own friend Liddon. Liddon, who later became a canon of St. Paul's in London, gave him the courage.

Clergymen of the Church of England are divided into three orders: deacons, priests, and bishops. A deacon is in Orders and may conduct services, preach, baptize, and marry men and women. He may assist a priest at the service, but he may not conduct Communion. Ordinarily a cleric of the English Church is first a deacon, then, when he has fulfilled certain obligations, becomes a priest.

Henry Liddon told Dodgson that a deacon was much freer than a priest and could regard himself as "practically a layman." With this encouragement, Dodgson decided to take deacon's Orders. He was ordained by the Bishop of Oxford on December 22, 1861.

He was now the Reverend Charles Lutwidge Dodgson, and with his formal broadcloth wore the turned-down starched white collar and white bow tie which were the badge of his profession. It was his clerical habit about Oxford, but also about Piccadilly, Covent Garden, the Haymarket, the Princess's, and others of his favorite London theatrical haunts. He had made a compromise which allowed him the best of two worlds: the advantages of the Church and preferment in Christ Church, and the freedom of not being fully committed to the restrictions placed on a parson. He had fulfilled the requirement of his studentship by "proceeding to Holy Orders." He never took priest's Orders. He preached and conducted services on occasion. He even baptized infants, but, as years later he wrote a nephew who was contemplating the priesthood, he never ceased to regard himself as "practically a layman."

54

Like his father, Charles Dodgson treasured a funny story. Already he had a reputation as a raconteur in the Hall and in the Senior Common Room, where Christ Church dons disported themselves in the evening and entertained their guests. Dodgson was deep in Christ Church as Student, Lecturer, editor of *College Rhymes*, and a member of the Choral Society of Oxford.

He was back and forth to the family home in Croft. He was in London more and more, for besides the theater he was cultivating the society of artists. He had suggested various jokes and humorous illustrations for *Punch*, got to know its editor, Tom Taylor, and through him various artists and London celebrities. Dodgson called on them, became friendly with them, and photographed as many of them as he could. He even transported all his equipment to London and set it up for a time in various borrowed studios and in the homes of his artist friends. At various times he took pictures of Holman Hunt, all the Rossettis, John Millais, Arthur Hughes, and other artists. His portraits of children and of the great were good enough so that he did not hesitate to place them on sale in Ryman's, an art dealer's shop in Oxford.

It was in the London studio of an artist named Munroe that he met the children of George Macdonald, the novelist, poet, and author of children's stories. They were a girl of six and a boy of seven. In serious discussion he convinced the small boy, who disliked having his hair combed, that he might be happier if he changed his head for a marble one. The idea appealed. The boy had very nearly decided that he would make the switch when he remembered that if he had a marble head he could not speak. He decided to keep the head he had.

When Dodgson paid this much attention to a small boy it was usually because the boy had a pretty sister. It was to Mary Macdonald that he wrote one of his "child letters," as he called them.

Now I want to know what you *mean* by calling yourself "naughty" for not having written sooner! Naughty, indeed! Stuff and nonsense! Do you think *I'd* call myself naughty, if I hadn't written to you, say for 50 years? Not a bit! I'd just begin as usual "My dear Mary, 50 years ago you asked me what to do for your kitten, as it had a tooth-ache, and I have just remembered to write about it. Perhaps the tooth-ache has gone off by this time — if not, wash it carefully in hasty-pudding, and give it 4 pin-cushions boiled in sealing-wax, and just dip the end of its tail in hot coffee. This remedy has never been known to fail." There! *That's* the proper way to write!

Affection, high spirits, cleverness, and a delicious absurdity sing in this Lewis Carroll letter to one of his earliest child friends.

Dodgson spent the morning of July 4, 1862, during the long vacation, with his photography. The Reverend F. H. Atkinson, who worked with him on *College Rhymes*, brought a visiting Mrs. and Miss Peters to his rooms, and Dodgson took pictures of them. They looked at his photograph albums and stayed to lunch. After Atkinson had taken his guests off to the museum, Dodgson gathered up the Reverend Robinson Duckworth and the three Liddell girls, Alice, Lorina, and Edith, and they started off for another of their excursions on the Isis.

This time they rowed upstream to Godstow instead of down to Nuneham. It was a beautiful, bright, sunny afternoon, and very warm. As usual, Dodgson was telling the girls stories as they slipped along through the glistening water of the calm stream. They kept clamoring for more, so the stories continued after they had abandoned their boat to take refuge in the shade of a hayrick on the bank of the river.

They were about three miles upstream and right in the country, with the nearest village a half-mile away. The towers and spires of Oxford, the spire of Christ Church among them, were all visible through the sunlit summer haze. The ruins of an old nunnery lay nearby. Occasionally a rabbit hopped past, for there were many rabbits about.

They had their tea on the riverbank and stayed there happily a long time, then started back to Oxford in the cool of the evening. It was a quarter past eight when they reached Christ Church again. They all went to Dodgson's rooms where they looked at his collection of microphotographs.

The story Charles Dodgson told the three small Liddells that summer afternoon was *Alice's Adventures Under Ground*. Long afterward, Robinson Duckworth remembered just how it happened. "I rowed *stroke* and he rowed *bow* in the famous long vacation voyage to Godstow, when the three Miss Liddells were our passengers, and the story was actually composed and spoken *over my shoulder* for the benefit of Alice Liddell, who was acting as 'cox' of our gig. I remember turning round and saying, 'Dodgson, is this an extempore romance of yours?' and he replied, 'Yes, I am inventing as we go along.' I also well remember how, when we had conducted the three children back to the deanery,

Alice said, as she bade us good-night, 'Oh, Mr. Dodgson, I wish you would write out Alice's Adventures for me.' He said he should try, and he afterwards told me he sat up nearly the whole night, committing to a MS. book his recollection of the drolleries with which he had enlivened the afternoon."

Many, many years later Alice remembered that afternoon on the Isis just as vividly, though after the passage of years, she remembered details differently. It was the next day, she said, that she started "to pester him to write down the story for me, which I had never done before. It was due to my 'going on, going on' and importunity that, after saying he would think about it, he eventually gave the hesitating promise which started him writing it all down."

No one had made notes. It didn't seem that important at the time. Not the children, not Duckworth, and not Dodgson himself realized the full significance of what had transpired on the river and on the river's bank that July afternoon. Just twenty-five years later, when *Alice in Wonderland* was one of the best-known books in England and in the United States and the story had just appeared on the stage, Dodgson gave his version how it all had happened.

> Many a day had we rowed together on that quiet stream — the three little maidens and I — and many a fairy tale had been extemporised for their benefit . . . yet none of these many tales got written down: they lived and died, like summer midges, each in its golden afternoon until there came a day when, as it chanced, one of my little listeners petitioned that the tale might be written out for her. . . . I distinctly remember, now as I write, how, in a desperate attempt to strike out some new line of fairy-lore, I

had sent my heroine straight down a rabbit-hole, to begin with, without the least idea what was to happen afterwards. . . . In writing it out, I added many fresh ideas, which seemed to grow of themselves upon the original stock; and many more added themselves when, years afterwards, I wrote it all over again for publication: but . . . every such idea and nearly every word of the dialogue, *came of itself.*

Five

Nothing comes out of a vacuum but the airlessness that is in it. A book does not come out of nowhere. Even as rare and wonderful a book as *Alice in Wonderland* has beginnings.

To Lewis Carroll the story seemed to come of itself. Duckworth thought the story flowed of itself through Dodgson's mind and into words that charmed the three listening children. The children knew that Dodgson was not making the story up through an effort of will. It was just something he knew and that he had always known and was telling them. They knew the story was true, not true because it was reasonable or in the way that the alphabet or a birthday is true, but true because, like a fact of nature, it existed. It was like the river. It was like the sunny afternoon. It was like themselves. It just was.

That was the kind of truth that Dodgson was telling, the truth of the river and the afternoon and the three children. He was telling the truth of his own childhood and of all he had read and remembered and imagined; the truth of his relationship with the three small girls, the truth of his Oxford life and the people he knew in it and the absurdities he relished. He was telling the truth of his own word-loving, pun-loving, puzzle-loving, fanciful, and logically precise mind.

Other people had known and told fairy tales long before Lewis Carroll. Animals had always talked in children's stories. When you are very young and the whole world is strange and exciting and you have hardly learned to talk yourself, it is just as reasonable to think that animals talk as that people do.

Dodgson knew stories like that. There were rabbits about them on the banks of the Isis. They all knew that other small animals and birds — mice, cats, pigs, hedgehogs, frogs — were all about them. Certainly they knew what a Lory was. That was Lorina. They knew who the Duck was; he was Duckworth. Better than anyone else, they knew the Dodo. When he went to say his name and stammered a trifle, Dodgson was Do-Dodgson. They all knew the kings, queens, and knaves in a pack of cards.

Dodgson had models for the wonderland he created. Everyone knew *Gulliver's Travels*. Sometimes Gulliver was a giant. That was in Lilliput, where the people were only six inches high. Sometimes he was a pygmy; that was in Brobdingnag, where the people were twenty feet tall, or whatever the height of that gigantic race was. There was sound precedent for Alice's being sometimes tiny and sometimes huge, though she went Gulliver one better and wrought the changes magically on herself.

61

Alice was not the first fictional character who had found herself the only human being in a strange land. Robinson Crusoe had been all alone on an island. None of them called him by it, but Dodgson and the children all knew that Duckworth's first name was Robinson. Without noticing, the storyteller may have got a hint from that and his listeners would have understood.

Other people had talked and written nonsense too. In none of his writing, not even in his diary or in his letters, does Charles Dodgson mention Edward Lear, but there are reminiscences of Lear in both the *Alice* books. Lear, at that time, was a very popular writer of humorous verse. He wrote so many limericks that people even called them Learicks and knew many of them by heart.

Born in 1812, thus twenty years older, Lear was like Dodgson an artist by temperament and talent. Unlike Dodgson, he became a professional painter, known for his landscapes in watercolor and in oil as well as for his humorous writings. Because of his precarious health — poor eyesight, chronic asthma, bronchitis, worst of all epilepsy — Lear spent most of his life abroad in Italy, Switzerland, France, and the Near East. Beginning as an illustrator of bird books, he had published five books of travel and painting before in 1846 he issued his first *Book of Nonsense*.

Like Dodgson, Lear was a bachelor. Like Dodgson with his stammer, he suffered a physical handicap. Like Dodgson he was an artist. Like Dodgson, he wrote nonsense, and it was more nonsensical nonsense than Dodgson's.

"How pleasant to know Mr. Lear!"

Lear had a big nose, a hideous visage, and a beard like a wig. He was perfectly round. He wore a runcible hat, and he wept by the sides of the ocean and on the top of the hill. He hated ginger beer, but he bought pancakes and lotion and chocolate shrimps from a mill. We have his word for all of this. He wrote learnedly of old men and odd women, seafaring owls and pussy-cats, tables, chairs, children, pelicans, geese, Jumblies, and the Yonghy-Bonghy-Bò.

> There was an Old Man with a beard
> Who said, "It is just as I feared! —
> Two Owls and a Hen,
> Four Larks and a Wren,
> Have all built their nests in my beard!"

All of Lear's other limericks are as moving and informative. They were relished and quoted in Oxford as in London. Undoubtedly Charles Dodgson knew them. When Lear is talking about an Old Person or a Young Person in Coblenz, Majorca, or West Dumpet, he is delightful and serene. When he is talking about toeless Pobbles, Calico Pie, or Quangle-Wangles, he is better than serene. He is blissfully idiotic.

Many shared the opinion of himself he expressed "by way of preface" to his *Book of Nonsense*.

> "How pleasant to know Mr. Lear!"
> Who has written such volumes of stuff!
> Some think him ill-tempered and queer,
> But a few think him pleasant enough.

Tennyson, who knew Dodgson well, was Lear's close friend and admirer. He wrote a laudatory poem to him, "To

E.L. On His Travels in Greece." John Ruskin was Dodgson's Oxford associate and adviser. In *The Pall Mall Magazine*, Ruskin wrote: "Surely the most beneficent and innocent of all books yet produced is the *Book of Nonsense* with its corollary carols — inimitable and refreshing, and perfect in rhythm. I really don't know any author to whom I am half so grateful, for my idle self, as Edward Lear. I shall put him first of my hundred authors."

Neither Tennyson nor Ruskin has left written comment on Lewis Carroll.

If Dodgson knew and owed a debt to Edward Lear, he never acknowledged it, and though he undoubtedly knew his books, Lear ignored Lewis Carroll. Both were intimates of Holman Hunt, William Rossetti, John Millais, and others of the Pre-Raphaelite painters. It is impossible they did not know of each other, but Lear's biographer suggests that Lear may have been jealous of the younger writer who had invaded his precincts. It is not improbable that Dodgson was likewise jealous of Lear.

There were merging literary influences behind Charles Dodgson that afternoon on the river, but more important to the creation of *Alice* were the time, the place, the circumstances, his experience, and his temperament.

The air was soft. The river was calm. They sky was blue. It was a serene and golden afternoon. "Golden" was Dodgson's own word for it. The river flowed gently by. There was the hum of insects over the grass. There were forget-me-nots along the stream, and the marsh flowers were in blossom.

There was ancient Oxford through the haze, and perhaps they could hear the distant sound of familiar Oxford bells. Dodgson faced the expectant children and his interested companion. The concatenation of circumstances was exactly right to bring out his will-o'-the-wisp imagination, the love of pun and parody, the delighted perception of absurdity, and set them all in flight. Charles Dodgson needed the fine weather, the admiration of the three girls, even the presence of Robinson Duckworth on that famous July Fourth excursion. He needed to have on his white flannels and boater straw rather than his clerical black. He needed to be well, to be happy, to come out with the Puck in him and the Ariel.

He had told the children many stories before. He had a store on which to improvise. His words poured out a mixture of what he had read, what he had experienced, and what he was. Probably he did not know at the time where an idea or this part of an idea came from, or the emotion which tinged his thought. He drew on Gulliver, Crusoe, perhaps on Lear. He drew on his long, lonely early childhood, on the days at Croft, on his experiences at Rugby, on what he knew, and in part they all knew, of the college and university world of Oxford. He drew on his emotions toward the children, particularly toward Alice, on his sensations of pleasure, on half-remembered games with his sisters. He utilized to the full the impulse and inspiration which came from all these sources and even the bodily pleasure he probably felt from the physical act of rowing their gig.

Lewis Carroll that July afternoon on the river was very conscious of Alice Liddell. He had been very conscious of her when he first saw her, when she was about three years old. Now she was ten. He saw not only the grave-faced child, but also perhaps the promise of the woman the child might become. Dodgson could see what he looked at, and because he was Lewis Carroll, because he was sensitive and imaginative, he sometimes saw more than was actually there to be seen. This was true when he looked at ordinary things about him and turned them into the completely ridiculous. It was true when he read a serious poem and wrote a parody of it more memorable than the poem itself. It certainly would be true when he looked at a small girl whose appeal he had felt from their first meeting.

Dodgson did not tell *Alice's Adventures Under Ground* and later write *Alice's Adventures in Wonderland* for children, but for a child. He wrote all of his Lewis Carroll writings always for some one girl child, and as much for himself as for the child. He was not an indiscriminate lover of children. He wrote for those small girls to whom he felt attracted. He wrote for himself because every writer writes for himself. He created fantasy that afternoon in response to feminine appeal, to an appreciative audience he wished to please and whose admiration the man needed, perhaps unconsciously, to evoke.

Charles Dodgson could not have created his story that afternoon unless his emotions had been stirred and his imagination aroused by something beyond the ordinary. He loved these children. In some way he loved Alice. He felt an elation, an upsurge of the spirit. Usually there must be the excitement of caring intensely about some one or some thing before the poetic impulse is stimulated to the point where a man can produce imaginative work of a high order. Mind alone cannot do it. The precise mathematician and pious young cleric of Tom Quad could never have been the author of *Alice* had it not been for the small girls.

An English Almanac describes the English countryside, the flowers, the birds, the weather, for each month and lists memorable dates. There is only one entry in it for July 4 of any year. Under 4th July 1862, Miles Hadfield wrote: ". . . during an expedition up the river to Godstow, the young Liddell sisters bewitched the Rev. C. L. Dodgson so that he became Lewis Carroll, who started telling them about the adventures of Alice." Dodgson had been Lewis Carroll for a long time, but the verb "bewitched" may well be accurate. Something, something of all the influences mentioned and more which slipped through his senses or rose from unconscious memories through his mind, worked magically on Charles Dodgson that afternoon.

He told the *Alice* story only in outline that afternoon. Not even Carroll could have extemporized the complicated puns and word play, the farcical illogicalities, and the verse parodies that appear in the finished work, but on the river and the river's bank he fused all the elements he could reach and use into the purest fantasy.

The story he told was satire as well as fantasy. The fairy tale has a clean and clear intellectual sting. That was for himself, and perhaps for Duckworth. It pointed swiftly to absurdities in people and in the use and misuse of words and ideas. Bright children have an acute sense of the absurd, and the children he spoke to were bright. Their perceptions were sharp and their opinions uncluttered by the prejudices and clouding uncertainties adults acquire. Dodgson's perceptions were sharp and his opinions uncomplicated too. The dancing appreciation of the wondrously absurd he had always had, and the children loved it. He filled his story with private jokes and intimate foolery they all understood. He put them all into the tale, not once but twice, then three times. If children always like a story, the story they like best is one about themselves. We are egoists by right of birth.

Ten-year-old Alice was the heroine, and it is easy to

imagine the delight with which she must have listened. It was her dream. It was she who lived through all the wondrous adventures and held her own with rabbits, mice, cats, kings, and queens. She cried occasionally underground, as anyone in all the predicaments she found herself in might be excused for doing, but she was brave all through. She gave as good as she got, but she was never unkind. Even when she was growing up and down at an alarming rate she maintained her dignity. In what is possibly the best piece written about Lewis Carroll, Walter de la Mare speaks of Alice's "saving good sense" and of her "sagacity of mind and heart." These were the qualities which Dodgson saw in Alice and which, listening, she knew happily that he saw.

Only two weeks before, the same five adventurers had sailed downriver to Nuneham, dined, walked about, and started home at four o'clock in the afternoon when a hard rain came pelting down. The drenched voyagers were forced to abandon ship and walk three miles through the rain to a house in Sandford where a Mrs. Broughton dried the children's sopping clothes and got the girls warm and dry while the two young clerics walked into Iffley and sent a light horse and carriage back for them. After they were all safely back in Dodgson's rooms, they had tea at about half past eight that evening.

In *Alice* this became the episode where Alice, a Duck, a Dodo, a Lory, and an Eaglet almost drown in the pool of Alice's own tears. In his editorial comments on Dodgson's diary, Lancelyn Green hazards the opinion that there might have been some joke at the time that Alice had brought on the rain at Nuneham through her tears, and that perhaps someone had said it was "raining cats and dogs" so dogs and cats too were floundering in the pool.

They all knew who the Twinkling Bat was. "Bat" was

the nickname of Oxford's Professor Bartholomew Price. They knew the Mad Hatter too. He was the same Theophilus Carter who had once eaten in Dodgson's Christ Church mess and now kept a furniture shop on the High. There were other characters in the tale whom they recognized, others who were like nobody they knew, still others who were like everybody they knew.

The Liddell girls laughed at the sly references to Miss Prickett and their lessons in reading, writing, and arithmetic which, of course, became reeling, writhing, and such branches of arithmetic as Distraction and Uglification in the Mock Turtle's school. They knew, too, that history lessons could be dry enough to dry you off no matter how wet you got.

Of course you grew up fast if you ate this or that — but not if you ate or drank that or this. Everybody was always telling them things like that. If eating a mushroom or a cake could make you grow to nine feet and eating something else shrank you to three inches, so much the better!

All the girls could sing "Star of the Evening," and they had sung it for Dodgson, but they liked his words for the popular song better:

> Beautiful Soup, so rich and green,
> Waiting in a hot tureen!

They knew the poem, "Speak Gently." Being small girls, they preferred the lullaby of the Duchess:

> Speak roughly to your little boy,
>   And beat him when he sneezes:
> He only does it to annoy,
>   Because he knows it teases.

70

What if the baby did turn into a pig? All little boys were pigs.

Then who should pop up but themselves again. They were not only in Dodgson's story, they were in the Dormouse's tale too, only now their names were Elsie (for L. C., Lorina Charlotte), Matilda (for Edith because that was her pet name), and Lacie (which is only an anagram for Alice). Alice was getting everything backward anyway. When she tried to recite

> "You are old, Father William," the young man cried,
> "The few locks which are left you are grey . . ."

the poem came out,

> "You are old, Father William," the young man said,
> "And your hair has become very white;
> And yet you incessantly stand on your head —
> Do you think, at your age, it is right?"

Alice went on and on in the story, and the poem grew more confused, as if she were in a dream — which she was — and had no control over what she said but heard it only after she had spoken.

They were all in a golden dream that afternoon: Dodo, the Duck, and Prima, Secunda, and Tertia, as Dodgson called the girls in the poem he later prefixed to his story.

"To please a child I loved (I don't remember any other motive)" Dodgson began to letter out his first recorded version of *Alice's Adventures Under Ground*. He lettered his manuscript instead of writing it in script because he thought it would be easier for Alice to read. Though Duckworth says that his friend stayed up most of that night

71

writing it down, Dodgson did not begin his finished manuscript until November 13. He hoped to finish it by Christmas.

He did not. It was not his careful lettering that took the time, but the illustrations. Ruskin had told Dodgson he had not talent enough to become an artist, and Dodgson was professionally untrained, but, if crude, the thirty-seven pictures drawn by the author for *Alice* have their own skill and vigor. They are well-intentioned but stiff. Dodgson could not capture Alice's face, which does not appear the same in any two of the illustrations. The one, full-length on the page, with Alice's neck accounting for about one-quarter of her height, is the most grotesque. It was at that point in the story where Alice was "opening out like the largest telescope that ever was." The real Alice, her serious child's face framed in straight dark hair, appears in a small oval photograph which Dodgson pasted at the end of the story.

Not until Saturday, November 26, 1864, more than two years after he had started it, could Dodgson deliver the manuscript book to Alice at the deanery.

There had been changes at the deanery. Another baby, named Albert Edward Arthur for the Prince of Wales, who was one of its godfathers, had been born and had died. A fifth daughter had been born in March 1864. Two months later, Dodgson was again being snubbed by Mrs. Liddell. May 12, 1864, he complains, "During these last few days I have applied in vain for leave to take the children on the river, i.e. Alice, Edith and Rhoda: but Mrs. Liddell will not let *any* come in future — rather superfluous caution." What had happened this time?

Perhaps, whatever it was, it had nothing to do with the children. Dodgson had had a tiff with the Dean about the awarding of junior studentships in Christ Church. Feeling that his authority had been in some way slighted, he had written his objections to the Dean. The Dean had replied saying he thought Dodgson's comments "hypercritical and unnecessary." Dodgson had persisted and made further protests.

Dodgson could be finicky, but the Dean and his wife had characteristics that several times made them the butt of Oxford satire. One quip was,

> I am the Dean, and this is Mrs. Liddell;
> She is the first and I the second fiddle.

The two main streets of Oxford are High Street and Broad Street. Both thoroughfares and university recognition of a certain amount of discernible self-satisfaction appeared in another rhymed barb:

> I am the Dean of Christ Church, Sir:
> This is my wife; look well at her.
> She's the Broad and I'm the High;
> We are the University.

Whatever the strained relationship may have been, *Alice's Adventures Under Ground* was received happily at the deanery.

According to one account, Henry Kingsley saw the manuscript book there and urged Mrs. Liddell to encourage Dodgson to publish it. Dodgson was doubtful. He asked Duckworth to read it and give him his opinion, saying he did not want to lose money having the book printed if it did not seem worthwhile. Duckworth, in turn, got his novelist friend George Macdonald to read it, and the response of all the Macdonald family was enthusiastic.

Thus encouraged, Dodgson began to write the story anew for publication. He managed to get Macmillan, publisher for the university, who had just successfully published Charles Kingsley's *Water Babies*, to accept the book on a commission basis. Dodgson would pay for the printing, illustrating, and engraving. Macmillan would handle the sales and pay him royalties. On the advice of Tom Taylor, Dodgson got John Tenniel, well-known political cartoonist, to agree to illustrate the book.

Dodgson knew that he was fortunate to get Tenniel, but he was more fortunate than he knew. Tenniel, who died Sir John Tenniel, was the chief political cartoonist for *Punch*. Blind in one eye as the result of a fencing accident, he drew with precision, grace, and penetrating humor. As a *Punch* artist he stood at the top of his profession, but he was more than a cartoonist. After winning an award for mural composition, he had done a large fresco for the Hall of Poets in the House of Lords. He had first come to wide public notice for his illustrations for *Aesop's Fables*. Tenniel was good, but neither his reputation, his skill, nor his courtesy could protect him from Charles Dodgson. Dodgson proceeded to send him mad.

A new side of the mathematician, expert photographer, and whimsical humorist came out now. Dodgson wanted something a bit better than perfection in the artwork for his exquisite book. He made suggestions to Tenniel. He wrote long criticisms of minute details in the sketches Tenniel submitted to him. He asked for major changes and for minor changes. He stabbed at Tenniel with his intensity. It was uncomfortable for the artist, but he never did better work. His illustrations for Lewis Carroll's book so perfectly complement the story that it would be hard to visualize *Alice's Adventures in Wonderland* — the new title which Dodgson finally adopted — without them.

The book was printed in Oxford, and the first copies were sent to Macmillan for distribution June 27, 1865. Dodgson ordered the very first copy to be sent to Alice Liddell so that she would receive it July 4, 1865, exactly three years after his telling her story on the Isis. The second copy, superbly bound in vellum, went to Princess Beatrice, eight-year-old daughter of Queen Victoria.

Dodgson sent out seventy presentation copies of *Alice*, and he made sure that many of these went to well-known writers and artists and to others whose opinions and influence would spread the fame and increase the sales of the little red book. Dodgson was a professional author now as well as a clergyman and a don, and he was sharply aware from the first of the practical aspects of authorship.

Production of *Alice* had cost him about 380 pounds (nearly $2,000 at the time). He wanted his money back and more with it, and, like every author, all the praise and fame he could get. He would not admit this even to himself. Quixotically, he drew a sharp line between the Reverend Charles Lutwidge Dodgson and Lewis Carroll. He insisted to the point of absurdity that others toe this line, but he did all he could always to push the literary pretensions of Carroll while as Dodgson he demurely demurred.

This time it was Tenniel who was dissatisfied and grew fastidious. As soon as he saw the book, he told Dodgson that the reproduction of his pictures was inferior and suggested a new printing. Most of the 2,000 copies of the first edition were withheld, and a second edition was produced in Oxford by a different printer. Dodgson saw the new run in November and was greatly pleased. He pronounced the second edition "very *far* superior to the old, and in fact a perfect piece of artistic printing."

Yet, meticulous as ever, he still found things in the book that he wished to change.

Dodgson's own copy of *Alice's Adventures in Wonderland* is now in the M. L. Parrish Collection in the library of Princeton University. The slim, squarish book is bound in dark red cloth with a head of Alice in a small circle stamped in gold on the front cover. Inside, on the upper right-hand corner of the half-title page of the book by Lewis Carroll, Dodgson drew his own monogram, CLD, in the form of a small circle. The text itself is unmarked, but on a blank page at the back Dodgson carefully listed in pen and ink thirty-seven corrections for any new printing. The corrections so crowded the small page that he had to write some vertically in the gutter margin.

He noted a broken letter, "r" in the word "for," on one page. He wanted more leading between the lines of several pages. He added commas — Dodgson always used plenty of commas, exclamation points, and italics. He made minor changes for the sake of the rhythm in a sentence here and there. In one place he decided to change "walk" to "go." He decided that the printer's rule above the book's dedication should be moved a trifle higher. He wanted infinitesimal changes in the mouse's tail. If, as some claim, genius is the infinite capacity for taking pains, Dodgson qualifies.

He was also a businessman. He heard of a chance to sell the discarded first-edition sheets in the United States. They were sent to New York, bound in red calico, and D. Appleton and Company distributed them in 1866. It was the first appearance of Alice and her oddly assorted friends in this country.

Six

If Charles Dodgson pronounced the November 1865 *Alice* a perfect piece of artistic printing, the reviewers did not know what to pronounce it at all. As there has never been a book quite like it since, there certainly had been no book like *Alice's Adventures in Wonderland* before.

Small wonder the reviewers were confused. This was a children's book. It was fantasy. It was a book of nonsense, a book of topsy-turvy incredibilities in which unreality took the place of reality and then somehow seemed more real than the real. It was a work of gentle and tender humor, of fondness and sentiment even, and then suddenly it wasn't. It was witty and satirical, and then it was absurd, just absurd. Fancy danced in it, but it danced in the spotlight of clear intelligence. That was the disconcerting part. So much was

77

completely logical, severely logical, without the comfortable concessions that most people make to illogicality as they live along. In a fantastic setting among unreasonable characters who said and did ridiculous things, Alice was often disturbingly reasonable.

The Athenaeum condemned the story as stiff and over-wrought. The *Illustrated Times* said it was so absurd that it irritated the reader. The *Illustrated News* praised it. The *Pall Mall Gazette* said it was the best of the children's books offered for sale that Christmas season, but *The Spectator* condemned the Mad Hatter. The reviewer could not know that he kept a furniture shop in the High and may have thought, Green suggests, that the Mad Hatter was a carica-ture of Gladstone. One publication had little use for the text but thought the book might get by because of Ten-niel's illustrations.

Alice's Adventures in Wonderland was never intended for very small children, a fact Dodgson acknowledged when later on he published a simplified *Nursery Alice* with enlargements of Tenniel pictures. The youngest of the three Liddell girls for whom he created the story was eight, Alice was ten, and Edith was thirteen. These were hardly infants.

It was a children's book in its clarity, its simple structure, and its simplicity of expression. These are the very qualities which appeal to adults as well as to children: a colorful, straightforward narrative, clearly told. Children could de-light in the talking animals, the dream world into which Alice tumbled, the animated pack of playing cards. Adults could enjoy all of these elements, then revel in the subtler meanings they could see or read into passages. Dodgson realized the truth that there is really little essential difference between the young, the older, and the old. At any age, the human mind and heart respond to the same delights.

Most of the great children's books have been written both for the enjoyment of children and the appreciation of adults. This is true of *Gulliver's Travels*. It is true of Kenneth Grahame's *Wind in the Willows*, where children can follow happily the story of the mole, the rat, the badger, and Mr. Toad and adults respond to the lyrical quality of the narrative as well as to the story. Adults as well as children applaud *Winnie-the-Pooh* and *Charlotte's Web*. The classic children's story has a universal and lasting appeal — which is what makes it a classic.

A few years ago a wise young instructor in philosophy always opened his college course in introductory logic by reading from *Alice in Wonderland*. What he read first was a bit of dialogue from the Mad Tea Party. The Mad Hatter, you remember, takes his watch out of his pocket, shakes it, puts it to his ear, then looks at it to see what day it is.

"Two days wrong!" sighed the Hatter. "I told you butter wouldn't suit the works!" he added, looking angrily at the March Hare.

"It was the *best* butter," the March Hare meekly replied.

"Yes, but some crumbs must have got in as well," the Hatter grumbled: "you shouldn't have put it in with the bread-knife."

The March Hare took the watch and looked at it gloomily: then he dipped it into his cup of tea, and looked at it again: but he could think of nothing better to say than his first remark, "It was the *best* butter, you know."

The syllogism here has gone askew, the instructor would happily point out. Premise does not lead accurately to conclusion in reasoning like this — only to the reader's delight. He would expatiate a little on the false reasoning at the tea party, then turn to the trial of the Knave of Hearts for a second apt example of illogicality and sweet Carrollian nonsense.

> "Take off your hat," the King said to the Hatter.
> "It isn't mine," said the Hatter.
> "*Stolen!*" the King exclaimed, turning to the jury, who instantly made a memorandum of the fact.

Alice in Wonderland is a textbook in logic by a skilled logician. It is also a poem, a poem in the sense that it speaks Dodgson's sense of what to him was lovely and of good report. It was a book about Alice for Alice. He saw the ten-year-old girl as loving and gentle, as loving as a dog (the comparison is his) and, like a princess, gravely courteous to everyone, King or Caterpillar: "courteous . . . then trustful, ready to accept the wildest impossibilities with all that utter trust that only dreamers know; and lastly, curious — wildly curious, and with the eager enjoyment of Life that comes only in the happy hours of childhood, when all is new and fair."

The White Rabbit, Dodgson meant as contrast to Alice. The Rabbit was old, timid, and quavering. He meant the Queen of Hearts to represent blind and aimless fury; the Red Queen to be as furiously unreasonable but pedantic and cold, "the concentrated essence of all governnesses," and the White Queen to be utterly stupid — fat, stupid, pale, and helpless.

For the rest, Dodgson meant many things in *Alice* but most of all nonsense — unadulterated, poetic, beautifully nonsensical nonsense just for the fun of it.

Humor comes in many shapes and sizes, some of the shapes as neatly formed as a bird and some of the shapes as shapeless as laughter itself. There are those to whom the funniest thing in the world is to see a man fall down and break his leg. Undoubtedly there is something funny about the ridiculous expression of mingled surprise and agony that contorts his face and the grotesque angle at which the shattered leg protrudes from his body. It is funny when someone pulls a chair out from under someone else who is about to sit on it. He looks incredulous and alarmed at the second when he realizes his plight and you see him bounce his pelvis on the floor. Sometimes you can hear it crack. As the early movie makers discovered, it is uproariously funny when someone gets a custard pie in the face. A pie-throwing scene can always provoke decibels of delighted risibility.

There is harsh cruelty in primitive humor of this kind. Perhaps there is cruelty in all humor, though fortunately the proportion in civilized humor, which generally is verbal, is considerably less. Crude humor depends largely on the predicament and discomfort of the butt of fate or a practical joke. Finer humor usually depends on recognition of the palpably absurd, perception of the delightfully unexpected, illogical, and improbable. It is relief from the ordinary, logical, and drab which the nonsensical and ridiculous afford.

Stephen Leacock, no mean humorist himself, pointed out that a child can and does laugh even before it can talk. As he saw it, laughter of this kind is a natural physical expression of well-being. After infancy, humor depends on seeing or hearing something that has suddenly ceased to be what you expect it to be, or a contrast between something as it ought to be and what it has unexpectedly changed into. A pumpkin is a pumpkin and no great cause for excitement. Hollow it out, cut slits for eyes, nose, and mouth, and it is a human head or face. It is funny or frightening on a dark Halloween night. Often what is funny is very near to what is frightening.

Alice plays croquet at the Queen of Hearts' garden party. She had played croquet before. So had most of the children who first read *Alice*. Ordinarily you use a wooden mallet to drive a large wooden ball through hooped wire wickets. In this game, the mallets were flamingoes, the balls were hedgehogs, and the wickets, soldiers bent over to form the hoops. This is ridiculous. It is funny. It tickles the imagination. You can visualize the scene, and yourself playing croquet as Alice had to play it with the Queen of Hearts.

It is funny, too, when the King decided on the instant that the Hatter has stolen the hat that isn't his. It is funny because the King is being stupid. He has jumped to a ridiculous conclusion. You feel superior to him and to all the others in *Alice* who make silly mistakes.

The distinction between wit and humor is fine. Often there is none, but wit is usually derisive. It mocks someone. It has sharpness and sting in it, and it makes a point of some kind. It depends upon mental agility and verbal cleverness, and the one who makes the quip and the reader who shares it feel superior to the one whose stupidity or dullness has laid him open to the jibe he deserves.

There is wit, stinging satire, amid all the gentleness of *Alice's Adventures in Wonderland*. The Queen's repeated, "Off with their heads!" is not only part of the violence which is also in the book, but a sharp comment on all those who solve their problems by easy and rather drastic measures.

There are sharp thrusts at the Oxford-academic way of stating simple things in the most pretentious and complicated way. The Duchess and Alice had been talking of mustard, and Alice decided that mustard was a mineral. The Duchess agreed and added that she had a large mustard mine nearby. "And the moral of that is — 'The more there is of mine, the less there is of yours.'" Then Alice decided that mustard was not a mineral but a vegetable.

> "I quite agree with you," said the Duchess; "and the moral of that is — 'Be what you would seem to be' — or, if you'd like it put more simply — 'Never imagine yourself not to be otherwise than what it might appear to others that what you were or might have been was not otherwise than what you had been would have appeared to them to be otherwise.'"

There is wit, but there is also simple comic playfulness: puns, riddles, word juggling, as in the play on "mine" in the dialogue between Alice and the Duchess. Wit is seldom kind. Humor of this innocent sort is seldom unkind.

Alice is the kind of humorous, witty, and nonsensical book that it is because Charles Dodgson was the kind of man he was. Humor is a subjective and individual quality. Had Dodgson been a dancer, a singer, a blacksmith, or a wigmaker instead of a mathematician and logician, his humor would have taken an entirely different form. Lewis Carroll had the characteristics of his Christ Church donnishness, but with them his inborn pleasure in the ludicrous, and his gift of language. The scholastic had overlaid but not smothered his boyish imagination, inventiveness, and readiness with words. Beneath his academic dignity and his mathematical scrupulosity was the *élan* of the boy who had gloried in performing magic tricks. His black gown and his subfusc hid but they had not extinguished his deftness of hand and mind.

Sense is commonplace. Most people have at least a little of it. It can be found almost anywhere and probably is for sale — on the installment plan — in the discount houses. Inspired nonsense is something else again. Only a few men have it, and one of these men was Charles Dodgson.

Sense is the attitude we ordinarily adopt toward the people and things around us. It is the way we make things intelligible and somehow get along. Sense lets us comfortably assume that two and two always make four, that apples are good to eat, and that no matter how much whipped cream you smear on it a lump of tar is generally inedible. Sense is orderly and safe. Nonsense is when we break through conventional common sense, decide that double the amount of the two halves of each or *pi r* square or a duet or just too too toot! toot! and look at the rascal go! Nonsense is not safe and dull but disorderly and capricious. It is escape from the mundane into the lunar and the lunatic. It makes puns, confusing "porpoise" with "purpose" and "soles and heels" with "soles and eels." It chooses one of the six other meanings of a word instead of the meaning indicated by sober context.

Yet nonsense is based on sense. It has to be. The human mind is so constituted that it cannot accept nonsense unless through sense. Mind looks for structure and meaning. That is why to some extent even nonsense must be sensible. Pure nonsense would not be understandable. It would be gibberish in a chaos. Dodgson's nonsense is understandable because behind it there is firm intelligence, and because in the *Alice* books he created a world where that nonsense is base, atmosphere, and pervading mental and emotional climate. All the reader has to do is fall into an ordinary rabbit hole with Alice, and there that world is and he can live in it.

It's all there — the nonsense, the story, the poetry, the humor, the wit, the logic, the fantasy, the pellucid intelligence. It is Lewis Carroll.

There is a confection that is sold at the annual spring garden show in Rittenhouse Square in Philadelphia. Perhaps it is sold elsewhere, but it has become traditional on this pleasant occasion in that pleasant place. The confection is a stick of lemon candy speared into a juicy lemon. You suck the sharpness of the lemon through the sweetness of the candy. It is deliciousness with a tang in it, honey with a tartness, a kind of tingling nectar. That is the taste of *Alice's Adventures in Wonderland*. The only other book with anything like the same taste is *Through the Looking-Glass and What Alice Found There*, which Lewis Carroll wrote six years later.

Seven

There is a familiar story, completely untrue, that Queen Victoria was so transported with *Alice in Wonderland* that she asked to have all the author's other books sent to her. When she got them, they turned out to be treatises on algebra, geometry, and logic, which was hardly what England's queen had expected. The story was told so often and became so widespread that Dodgson went out of his way to deny it wholly, emphatically, and in detail in the postscript of the "Advertisement" prefaced to his *Symbolic Logic*. It is too bad, for it is the kind of story which should have been true.

A less amusing but more touching story of the queen and *Alice* was told by Walter de la Mare. In 1866, still in deep mourning for Prince Albert who had died five years before, Queen Victoria was talking with one of her ladies at Windsor. The lady's small girl of three and a half sat on a footstool near a fire turning the pages of *Alice's Adventures in Wonderland*. Suddenly she jumped up and ran to the queen to show her Tenniel's picture of Alice swimming desperately in the pool of her own tears. "Do you think, please, you could cry as much as that?" she demanded.

A hush fell over the room where all the ladies present at the tea table sat embarrassed and fearful of the queen's reaction. It was the queen who broke the silence with what de la Mare's informant, who could not recall her actual words, described as "so ardent a tribute to Carroll that even Dodgson might have welcomed it." The next day a special palace messenger brought the little girl a small locket with intertwined horseshoes in coral and seed pearls and a miniature picture of the queen inside.

Dodgson should have overheard, for he worshipped his queen. He had already heard from her indirectly in words that warmed him.

"Heard from Mrs. Read," he wrote in his diary on Sunday, May 1, 1864, "enclosing a letter from Lady A. Stanley to Lady A. M. Dawson in which she says that she has shown my photographs to the Queen, and is commanded to say that 'Her Majesty admires them very much. They are such as the Prince would have appreciated very highly and taken much pleasure in'." Queen Victoria could have bestowed no higher praise.

Dodgson had bought a new camera. He was so busy with his teaching that the college gave him a grant of thirty-five pounds a year to pay for an assistant. He was often in London, staying overnight with some of his family or

putting up at the Old Hummel or the Great Northern, and seeing whatever was on the boards at the Lyceum or the Olympic, Covent Garden, the Princess's. He saw Ellen Terry in every play in which she appeared.

One evening he had "five hours of unmixed enjoyment" from what was certainly a mixed bill: *Hamlet;* then *The Maid and the Magpie, or the Fairy Paradise;* then *Hanky Panky, the Enchanter.* One other July evening, in the year *Alice* was published, he sat through *The Girl I Left Behind Me* (the Civil War was going on in the United States); *The Serf, or Love Levels All,* a drama set in Russia; and *Simpson & Co.,* a two-act comedy.

In court in Oxford he approved a long and clever speech by a man who was being tried for sheepstealing. A burglar who had robbed an alderman's house got six years. If the burglar also made a speech, Dodgson had no comment on it.

Dodgson was dining in Hall, dining in, and dining out. He invited dinner guests to his college rooms, where they were served from the famed Christ Church kitchens. He was very fond of entertaining and as precise and fastidious about it as he was about every other phase of his life. Sometimes he had large dinner parties, sometimes a single guest, but he always kept a diagram of the seating and of the menu so that he would not offer the same people the same dishes too frequently.

His stock had gone up in the Common Room. The dull lecturer and prim cleric had written a small book of wit

Her Majesty admires Mr. Dodgson's photographs very much.

and humor that was becoming widely appreciated. His fellows were surprised and a little taken aback. Some were pleased; others were jealous. Dodgson, the acknowledged wit and raconteur, sometimes sparkling, sometimes aloof and cold and no raconteur at all, was incomprehensible.

They all knew he had written *Alice*, and he knew that they knew it, and he was pleased. It also pleased him neither to affirm nor deny the book's authorship. He refused to be known as Lewis Carroll and would not acknowledge the name as written or verbal address. He was indignant when anyone referred to him as the author of *Alice* and pointed out sharply that the Reverend C. L. Dodgson did not admit authorship of any book which he had not signed. It was an anomalous position he assumed, and he did not assume it out of the playfulness of Lewis Carroll but out of the piety of the Reverend C. L. Dodgson and the dignity of C. L. Dodgson, M.A., Student and Lecturer of the proudest college in England's oldest and proudest university.

He may have thought the publication of a book of nonsense for children a little *infra dig* for an Oxford don and realized that the book's success made the offense that much worse. The academic scholar is expected to write and publish learned papers in connection with his studies. Dodgson knew what was expected of him, and he was doing that too.

He was a compulsive writer. He was always writing serious or comic verse, sketches, letters for publication, polemics on university problems, books and papers on some aspect of mathematics. This was his profession, and he found it no hardship. He loved mathematics as he loved puzzles, riddles, exercises in logic, and anagrams. They were all part of the same game for him, and it was a game he was good at.

He had already published books on algebra, geometry, and trigonometry. He made his professional standing secure with his *Condensation of Determinants* (1866), his *Elementary Treatise on Determinants* (1867), *The Fifth Book of Euclid Treated Algebraically so far as it relates to Commensurable Magnitude* (1868), and his *Algebraical Formulae for Responsions* (1868). Many more treatises followed in later years.

Most of these books were as dry as the history books he mocked in *Alice* and as scientific as the pure mathematics which was his subject. Once, though, the Lewis Carroll in Charles Dodgson broke loose in a tightly disciplined field. He wrote *Euclid and His Modern Rivals* in the form of a Platonic dialogue between Minos and Rhadamanthus, with the ghost of Euclid appearing every now and then like that of Hamlet's father. The argument was serious, but not always Dodgson's presentation of it. At one point bored Minos falls asleep. At another, he insists on discussing the center of gravity of a flea, and Herr Niemand (the ghost of a German professor who "has read all books and is ready to defend any thesis, true or untrue") is shocked and indignant.

His fantasies, his always voluminous correspondence, and his mathematical writing should have kept Dodgson fully occupied. They did not suffice. He became as prolific a writer on logic and on university affairs.

Christ Church and Oxford were always pulsating with controversies, and Charles Dodgson was a born controversialist. His pen was always ready and poised like a dart to prod the authorities and his university fellows. A conservative politically, socially, and religiously, he was against change, against change of any kind. He struck at change whenever it reared its restless head. Like the Queen of Hearts, he would gladly have lopped it off. That, perhaps, is where the Queen got her idea. Dodgson loved to go snicker-snack in Oxford with his vorpal blade, and he wielded it unstintingly.

The wonder is that his photography left him time for any of this. Photography was not a hobby with Charles Dodgson. It was an obsession. He ate and slept photography. As Tennyson had surmised, he probably dreamed it.

Dodgson had failed in his attempt to photograph Prince Albert. He succeeded in getting Prince Frederick of Denmark for "a victim," as he called his subjects, and photographed the prince in his Oxford undergraduate's cap and gown. "He conversed pleasantly and sensibly and is evidently a much brighter specimen of royalty than his brother-in-law." Dodgson had got even with Prince Albert! He also took Prince Leopold, Victoria's youngest son. Princes, knights, lords, and earls were the subjects Dodgson liked for portraiture. If they had no titles, his sitters at least had to have achieved eminence of some kind. Dodgson did not court the society of nobodies.

John Ruskin sat for him. So did Max Müller, Oxford's noted professor of philology, Canon Liddon, Dean Stanley, Michael Faraday, and other academicians. He took Dante Gabriel, Christina, and William Rossetti with their mother and in individual portraits. He took John Tenniel. He took his friend Tom Taylor of *Punch* and any number of clergy-

Photography was not a hobby with Dodgson. It was an obsession.

men, usually those of rank: the Archbishops of Canterbury and York, the Bishops of Lincoln, Ripon, and Oxford. One of his favorite novelists, Charlotte Yonge, sat for him. He posed his favorite actress, Ellen Terry, more than once — posed all of the Terry family. He took Lord Salisbury in his ornate robes as Chancellor of Oxford, with a small son reclining on his lap and another upright by his side.

The eminent posed willingly for him, often holding a pose from forty-five seconds to a minute and a half, sometimes with their heads clamped in a photographer's headrest. Few of them suspected that the world would forget most of them and remember only the photographer.

Carroll took thousands of pictures, taking infinite pains with composition and background to achieve just the effects he wished. He used plates of five different sizes, from 8 by 10 inches down to 3¼ by 4¼ inches. He had to coat the wet plates, then develop them while they were still wet. Everything had to be handled with great deftness, kept free of dust, and not allowed to touch anything. He had to develop his plates by pouring the proper solutions over them while he held them balanced in his other hand. He had to print, tone, and fix his own positives. Some printing he had done by commercial firms. As Dodgson practiced it, photography was art and almost legerdemain.

Important people were one of his two classes of subjects. The other, even nearer and dearer to the Reverend C. L. Dodgson, was small girls.

He took Alice Liddell again and again. There is an odd note in his diary for May 11, 1865: "Met Alice and Miss Prickett in the quadrangle: Alice seems changed a good deal, and hardly for the better — probably going through the awkward stage of transition." It was a passing mood, one of the dark moods that often came over him. He photographed Alice every time he could get permission. He was photographing her as late as June 25, 1870, when she was eighteen years old. There was a reason. It was the day on which he had been photographing Lord Salisbury, the Chancellor, a Christ Church man who became England's Foreign Secretary, then twice Prime Minister. Only too anxious to do as the Chancellor did, Mrs. Liddell hurried Alice and Ina into Dodgson's studio.

Any attractive small girl Dodgson sighted on the street, on the train, in The Parks or anywhere about Oxford, he saw as a subject. He posed the small daughters of his friends in his rooms or in a room in Badcock's yard near St. Aldgate's which, in 1863, he rented for his work. One favorite child subject was Xie Kitchin. Once Dodgson, who was not in the habit of joking about his photography, asked the artist Henry Holiday if he knew how to take a perfect photograph. When Holiday admitted that he did not, Dodgson said, "Take a lens and put Xie before it."

Xie was the small daughter of Dr. George William Kitchin, Student of Christ Church and Mathematical Examiner, who became Dean of Durham and of Winchester. Dodgson took Xie first dressed in rags, the next year in Indian shawls and a red petticoat and then in Greek dress. A few years later he posed her lying full length in a long nightgown on a sofa and declared this his best picture of her. He took pictures of Xie over a period of eleven years and long after she had ceased to be a child.

He had a cupboard full of costumes, some of which he borrowed from friends and museums, in which to pose his little girls. He posed them with dolls or carrying spears and wearing helmets. He posed them with croquet mallets or rope ladders, as Turks or Chinese. He even took story pictures. "The Elopement" showed small Alice Jane Donkin, in a cape and carrying a basket or bundle, about to descend a rope ladder from her window. He took Robert Bickersteth, Bishop Bickersteth's son, in a Volunteer uniform with his sister Florence crying on his shoulder, and called it "The Soldier's Farewell."

Day after day and all day Dodgson spent happily in his studio and darkroom, but even photography was put aside for three months of the long vacation of 1867. The camera, chemicals, darktent, and all the rest were too cumbersome to pack and carry. For the first and last time in his life Dodgson left England. With his friend, the Reverend Henry Liddon, he set out on what was then, as for different reasons it is now, a considerable journey. They went to Russia.

The priest and the deacon in their clerical black set out from London. Dodgson, coming in from the north, arrived in the city at Paddington. The Sultan of Turkey, who happened to reach London on the same day, arrived at Charing Cross. "I must admit," Dodgson reported dryly, "that the crowd was greater at the latter place." He met Liddon at a Dover hotel on July 13, 1867.

> We breakfasted, as agreed, at 8 — at least we sat down & nibbled bread & butter till such time as the chops should be done, which great event took place at about ½ past. We tried pathetic appeals to the wandering waiters, who told us "they are coming, Sir" in a soothing tone — and we tried stern remonstrances, & they then said, "they are coming, Sir" in a more injured tone; & after all such appeals they retired into their dens, & hid themselves behind sideboards and dish-covers, & still the chops came not.

It might have been yesterday instead of more than a century ago. Dodgson's idea was either to leave without paying or to complain to the manager, "which would certainly have produced a general row, if not the chops," but Liddon managed to quiet his impatient companion. Evidently they eventually got some kind of breakfast, for they boarded the channel steamer for France in a hard rain. Despite the example set by fellow tourists, they did not get seasick during the hour-and-a-half crossing.

The thirty-five-year-old Charles Dodgson was once more the eager and indefatigable sightseer on the whole of their tour, which took them into France, Belgium, and Germany as well as Russia. Liddon was partly on official business, commissioned to examine the state of the Russian Orthodox Church. Dodgson looked at every church in every city and town they went to because he was a churchman, was used to churches in Oxford, and because, like the Alps or the Taj Mahal, they were there to be looked at.

Dutifully he described them all in his *Journal of a Tour in Russia in 1867*, but he was more interested in other buildings and in activities for which his passion was unabated. Everywhere they went the two clerics located the theaters, found out what was playing, and whether or not they understood the language, attended every performance for which they could obtain tickets.

Dodgson saw so many churches in Cologne that he left with no definite idea of any of them. In Berlin they visited a Jewish synagogue, a novel experience for him. In Danzig it was a bird that took his eye. "At the hotel was a green parrot on a stand: we addressed it as 'pretty Poll,' & it put its head on one side & thought about it, but wouldn't commit itself to any statement. The waiter came up to inform

97

us of the reason of its silence — 'Er spricht nicht English: er spricht nicht Deutsch.' It appeared that the unfortunate bird could speak nothing but Mexican! Not knowing a word of that language, we could only pity it."

Between the Russian frontier and St. Petersburg the peasants looked dull to Dodgson, and the churches, each circular dome surrounded by four smaller ones painted green, looked like cruet stands. His tone changed when they reached Moscow.

> We gave 5 or 6 hours to a stroll through this wonderful city, a city of white & green roofs, of conical towers that rise one out of another like a foreshortened telescope; of bulging gilded domes, in which you see as in a looking-glass, distorted pictures of the city; of churches which look, outside, like bunches of variegated cactus . . . and which, inside, are hung all round with Eikons & lamps, & lined with illuminated pictures up to the very roof; & finally of pavement that goes up & down like a ploughed field, & droshky-drivers who insist on being paid 30 per cent extra today "because it is the Empress' birthday."

At the Treasury they saw so many crowns, thrones, and jewels that they seemed to Dodgson more common than blackberries. They went to a Russian wedding. They went through the palace. They ate what Dodgson called villianous food. They wandered through the fairs buying ikons. They saw the Persian and Chinese quarters. Then they went to the theater, and Dodgson was transported. At the Nijni they saw a burlesque of Aladdin and the Wonderful Lamp, and Dodgson was delighted with the play and with the acting. Later at the same theater he saw *Cochin China* and *The Hussar's Daughter*. A few nights later at Moscow's Little Theater they saw *The Burgomaster's Wedding* and *A Woman's Secret*.

Dodgson tried his hand at sketching the interior of a peasant cottage and a group of six peasants, but did not succeed too well. Waiters proved as recalcitrant in Russia as everywhere else, but the droshky drivers were worse.

Aug. 20 (Tu.) After a hearty breakfast, I left Liddon to rest & write letters, & went off shopping, &c. beginning with a call on Mr. Muir at No. 61 Galerne Ulitsa. I took a droshky to the house, having first bargained with the driver for 30 kopeks (he wanted 40 to begin with). When we got there we had a little scene, rather a novelty in my experience of droshky-driving. The driver began by saying "sorok" (40) as I got out: this was a warning of the coming storm, but I took no notice of it, but quietly handed over the 30. He received them with scorn & indignation, & holding them out in his open hand, delivered an eloquent discourse in Russian of which "sorok" was the leading idea. A woman who stood by with a look of amusement & curiosity perhaps understood him. I didn't, but simply held out my hand for the 30, returned them to the purse, & counted out 25 instead. In doing this I felt something like a man pulling the string of a shower-bath — & the effect was like it — his fury boiled over directly, & quite eclipsed all the former row.

I told him in very bad Russian that I had offered 30 once, but wouldn't again: but this, oddly enough, did not pacify him. Mr. Muir's servant told him the same thing at length & finally Mr. Muir himself came out and gave him the substance of it sharply & shortly — but he failed to see it in a proper light. Some people are very hard to please.

As publishers, artists, printers, and engravers found out, the Reverend C. L. Dodgson was not an easy man to deal with when pounds, pence, or kopeks were involved.

The travelers went to Warsaw. They fought with a waiter in Giessen, Germany. They strolled about the cities in France. They inspected cathedrals and gambling casinos. They heard concerts and saw pictures. On September 13 they sailed from Calais for England. Dodgson stood on the bow of their channel steamer chatting with the sailor on watch and searching for the lights of Dover "as they slowly broadened on the horizon, as if the old land were opening its arms to receive its homeward bound children." The continent had its points, but Lewis Carroll preferred voyaging on the Isis with his child friends.

Soon after his return to Oxford, Dodgson's life was marked by events of major importance in his career. These might not have stood out in the more eventful life of a man of action. To the scholar-humorist-photographer-clergyman who spent his entire mature life safely insulated from the rough-and-tumble of the Victorian world in his college tower, they were landmarks.

In June 1868 Archdeacon Dodgson died. Though Carroll was now thirty-six and his father had been sixty-eight, the death of the formidable cleric on whom he had modeled his religious ideas and his deportment was a severe blow. The home at Croft was broken up, and in August the family took a home named the Chestnuts in Guildford, the county town and chief market town of Surrey, some twenty-nine miles south of London.

That same year Carroll moved into the suite of rooms, one of the best in Christ Church, which had been Lord Bute's. This was to be his home for the rest of his life. On the first floor in the northwest corner of Tom Quad he had four sitting rooms, two bedrooms, a lobby, and a store-room. More of his rooms were in the little turrets over-looking St. Aldgate's, and from his upper floor he could easily reach the flat college roof. He hung his large study with oil paintings by artists whose work he admired. In this room the shelves were stocked with his considerable library of mathematical, medical, and literary works. His volumi-nous papers he arranged in neatly labeled pigeonholes.

It was in these commodious quarters on Staircase 7 that Dodgson entertained his frequent dinner guests and his child friends. He felt himself perfectly equipped when he obtained permission from the college authorities to build a new photographic glasshouse and studio on the roof.

In the cabinets of his study were all the toys and games he used to entertain his little girl guests. He played games with them, told them stories, puns, and riddles, then from under his bookshelves he got out his furry black bear that walked when it was wound, or one of the many different kinds of dolls or all of them. In the same hiding place were fourteen different music boxes and an orguinette, with a handle like a barrel organ, that played when perforated sheets were fed into it. Sometimes, for their greater amuse-ment, Dodgson inserted these sheets backwards, and the little girls laughed at the odd sounds that spilled out.

Then came the fun of scrambling into whatever cos-tumes they were to pose in and going out into the studio, which was often very hot, to be arranged in groups or a picture story or just posed alone until the photographer had got everything just right. There was the ordeal of sitting very still while he took the pictures. Sometimes after Dodgson had disappeared into his mysterious darkroom from which the smell of collodion drifted out, his sitters were allowed to go out on the roof and look at the towers of Oxford as reward for their endurance.

Dodgson believed in work. Work was his refuge from any emotional upset. He worked harder than ever the year of his father's death. Sometimes it seems as if he found work a refuge from life itself, and there are those who attribute at least part of his tense activity to disappointment with what, in some department, life had offered him or he was emotionally equipped to take.

In 1869 Dodgson published *Phantasmagoria and Other Poems*. He called it a collection of poems grave and gay. The poems had first appeared in various publications. The grave poems in the book are moralistic, commonplace, and sometimes mawkishly sentimental. The gay poems cannot match the wit and humor of his verse elsewhere. One poem was "Hiawatha's Photographing." As Dodgson admitted, Longfellow was easy to parody, and Dodgson certainly knew his subject.

> From his shoulder Hiawatha
> Took the camera of rosewood,
> Made of sliding, folding rosewood;
> Neatly put it all together....

Dodgson was a genius only sometimes, and certainly not in *Phantasmagoria*, but he was already at work on the second of his matchless Lewis Carroll books.

Alice's Adventures in Wonderland was doing well in the market. Two years after publication, Dodgson had cleared more than 250 pounds over the cost of producing the book. It continued to sell well, bringing him a small but steady income. Even before this time, Dodgson had planned a sequel. In January 1867 he had asked the artist Richard Doyle, formerly of *Punch*, uncle of Conan Doyle and a close friend of the Tennysons, if he would illustrate some new *Alice* stories for him.

Doyle liked the idea but feared he could not get the pictures done on time, so Dodgson went back to Tenniel. June 18, 1868 (three days before the death of Archdeacon Dodgson), Tenniel warily agreed to undertake illustrating a second *Alice* book, and Dodgson began to work out his ideas. He drew on pieces he had written at Croft more than a dozen years before and on other tales he had told Alice Liddell, and began to work his material into a form comparable to but distinct from that which he had used in the original *Alice*.

He was doggedly lecturing. He was briskly writing more of his mathematical books and pamphlets. He now spent vacations with his sisters at Guildford in the south of England instead of at Croft in Yorkshire. He invented a new telegraph cypher. He got his brother Skeffington established as curate to a rector whom he knew. He wrote the manager of the Covent Garden Theatre advising him how to regulate the after-performance carriage traffic. He went to Nottingham to try still another cure for his stammering; he had tried several already. He preached regularly to the servants of the college at services held for them and, as deacon, sometimes assisted at Holy Communion. He urged mothers to bring nightgowns in which to pose their small daughters when they visited his studios. He had already begun the experiment of photographing his small subjects in less. His every moment seems to have been filled, but he was working with all his concentrated and crystallized power on his new story for and about Alice Pleasance Liddell.

He dedicated his new tale to Alice Liddell, "Child of the pure unclouded brow," and appended a poem in which the initial letters of the lines spell out her name, but it was another Alice who helped give him his looking-glass idea.

Carroll had always been fascinated by the inverse and the reverse. He liked to play at upside down and inside out. He wrote letters backward so that they had to be read in a mirror. He talked amusingly to child friends about left and right, supplanting one meaning of "right" with another and doing the same with "left." Once in London when he was staying with one of his uncles, Carroll called out to Alice Raikes, a distant young cousin of Alice Liddell who lived close by, and asked her help in explaining something which, he said, had puzzled him for a long time. He took her inside, placed her in front of a tall mirror with an orange in her hand, asked her which hand she held it in, and whether the girl in the mirror held the orange in her right or left hand.

Alice Raikes in *The Times*, January 22, 1932, when the centennial of Carroll's birth was observed, told of trying to solve the problem. "I couldn't explain it, but seeing that some solution was expected, I ventured, 'If I was on the *other* side of the glass, wouldn't the orange still be in my right hand?' I can remember his laugh. 'Well done, little Alice,' he said. 'The best answer I've had yet.'"

So this time, instead of sending his heroine down a rabbit hole, Dodgson sent her through a looking-glass into the re-

104

verse and bewildering world she found there in the society of kings, queens, knights, gnats, Tweedledum, Tweedledee, Humpty Dumpty, walruses, carpenters, oysters, hundreds of talking flowers, and one, just one, Jabberwock.

Henry Liddon, his companion in Russia, now a canon of great St. Paul's in London as well as a professor at Oxford, gave him the title: *Through the Looking-Glass and What Alice Found There.*

Lewis Carroll finished the new book January 4, 1871. It was published December 6 of the same year. *Alice in Wonderland* was firmly established now, with Macmillan reporting large sales at every Christmas season. The bookstores took 8,000 copies of *Through the Looking-Glass* even before Carroll received his own copies. The original printing of 9,000 copies was sold so quickly that 6,000 more had to be printed even before the book was fairly under way.

The critics had something to go by this time, and their reviews were enthusiastic. Readers liked it too. Collingwood tells the story of his uncle's asking a small girl if she had read both his *Alice* books. He got his answer: "Oh, yes, I've read both of them, and I think" (this more slowly and thoughtfully) "I think 'Through the Looking-Glass' is more stupid than 'Alice's Adventures.' Don't you think so?"

Lewis Carroll must have been pleased. He knew that by "stupid" his small critic meant nonsensical and fantastic, and he may have shared her prejudice. Many have their favorite in either *Alice* or the *Looking-Glass*, but the two stories are from the same cloth. The delights of one are the delights of the other. As in *Alice*, Carroll is free. The skittering fancy, the ingenuity, the implacable logic, the lighted intelligence are all in play again. The Ariel, the sprite, and the mischievous Puck in Carroll are at large once more, though their abandon is all within the rules of the game. This time it is not, as it is in *Alice*, a pack of cards, but Alice and chessmen moving about the chessboard in the precise fashion dictated by the rules of chess.

It is in *Through the Looking-Glass*, of course, that Carroll expanded the "stanza of Anglo-Saxon verse" he had written in 1855 into the famous "Jabberwocky" which only Humpty Dumpty could explain. It is in the *Looking-Glass*, too, that

> The Walrus and the Carpenter
> Were walking close at hand:
> They wept like anything to see
> Such quantities of sand:
> 'If this were only cleared away,'
> They said, 'it *would* be grand!'

It was not the sand which got cleared away but the unsuspecting oysters who got done in.

One of the most appealing characters — for which Tenniel did one of his best illustrations — is the White Knight with his gentle face, shaggy hair, and large mild eyes. His person and his steed are so hung about with gadgets and inventions that he cannot remain upright in his saddle but is continually falling off one side or the other of his horse. Some readers have thought the White Knight to be Lewis Carroll's nonsense picture of himself.

The White Knight's mind goes on working all the time. He can't stop it. He is a wonderful hand at inventing things. None of them work, and he doesn't really expect them to work, and his ideas are as impractical as they are implausible, but Alice loves him and tries her best to comfort him. Even though she has heard so much strange poetry that

106

day, she even listens patiently to his long ballad about the aged man sitting on his gate.

In answer to his repeated questions about what he does, the old man tells the White Knight,

> . . . I hunt for haddocks' eyes
>   Among the heather bright,
> And work them into waistcoat-buttons
>   In the silent night.
>
> I sometimes dig for buttered rolls,
>   Or set limed twigs for crabs:
> I sometimes search the grassy knolls
>   For wheels of Hansom-cabs.

It was a long sad song the White Knight sang. Alice listened gently to the end. Then the Knight pointed her way but asked her to wait and see him off. "I shan't be long. You'll wait and wave your handkerchief when I get to that turn in the road? I think it'll encourage me, you see."

Alice waited, watching him fall off his laden steed — the horse wore anklets of the Knight's contriving to protect him from shark bites — five times before he and his deal box and the bunches of candlesticks, carrots, and fire irons he had tied to his saddle reached the turn. She waved her handkerchief, and went on to become a queen in the world beyond the looking-glass.

There is a sadness in *Through the Looking-Glass*. It is expressed early in "Child of the pure unclouded brow," which is tender, nostalgic, and yearning. The story itself is even more ingenious and filled with more abstruse byplay than *Alice in Wonderland*. It is more cunningly wrought. It lacks some of the summer sunniness of *Alice*, and it has discernible bitterness in it; not harsh bitterness, but the kind of bitterness of the nut inside a peach or plum stone.

The *Looking-Glass* is almost a panoplied display of Carrollian virtuosity. The wit and the precision of the humor seem more exact, yet there is a greater sureness and lift to the poetry. Dodgson's nonsense verse reaches it's apex, and the apex of nonsense verse in English, with the "Jabberwocky." There is a masterly sureness about it and about the other nonsense verse in the book.

When Humpty Dumpty used a word, it meant just what he chose it to mean, neither more nor less. He said so. When Lewis Carroll used words in the two *Alice* books, they might mean all sorts of things, all the sorts of things that anybody could mean by using them, and always more rather than less. In the *Looking-Glass* he tosses them in showers to sparkle in the light, pinks with them like a skilled swordsman, and uses them to construct his own kind of cunningly logical illogicalities. It is a performance contained within the precise limits he set for himself by the chess pattern of his tale, just as a poet sets restraints to the expression of his emotion in the strict form of the sonnet. Perhaps because of this, the *Looking-Glass* seems less fluid, more brittle, than *Alice in Wonderland*. The delicacy is a trifle more rigid.

This is splitting hairs. It is akin to the activity of those who amaze themselves by finding too many symbolic and tortured meanings in the two *Alice* books, more usually in the second book than in the first. Most of them would have surprised the author.

Lewis Carroll created two new worlds. One of them any wondering child may find at the bottom of any rabbit hole or treacle well. He can catch a tantalizing glimpse of the other every time he looks into a mirror. Carroll painted wondrously the absurdities that make life magical for little girls and supportable for unicorns and most of the rest of of us. Sir Philip Sidney was a Christ Church man almost three hundred years before Charles Lutwidge Dodgson. In Sidney's words, Lewis Carroll, in his two *Alice* books, comes "with a tale which holdeth children from play, and old men from the chimney corner."

Eight

Ralph Waldo Emerson was in England in 1874. The most important literary man in the United States, he mingled with the great in London: Robert Browning, John Stuart Mill, Gladstone, James Anthony Froude, the Duke of Argyle, Thomas Hughes. From April 30 to May 3 he was the guest in Oxford of Professor Max Müller. He met John Ruskin, Benjamin Jowett, and other university dignitaries. Prince Leopold lunched with him at the Müllers', then took Emerson to his own rooms for tea and to show him the pictures in his photograph album.

Emerson was a swell and mingled with the swells of the university. The next night, with his daughter Ellen, he dined with Dean Liddell, now Vice-Chancellor of the university, and a large company. It may have been at the Liddells that Emerson, as he recorded in his journal, met "Mr. Dodgson, author of *Alice in Wonderland*."

Charles Dodgson was not one of the swells of Oxford, but he was now a celebrity and Christ Church was sedately proud of him. He was trotted out for distinguished guests, and when they dined in Hall or at a private dinner party he was usually placed next to the visitor because of his wit and his well-known abilities as a storyteller. He seemed to have an inexhaustible fund of funny stories, and he told them well.

Dodgson was gregarious. The college was his life. It was very nearly all the life he had. It was important to him, and he was intensely concerned with the university and The House. Never a recluse, he was dependent on the society of his academic fellows. He needed people around him, something going on. When he found himself alone in Oxford during part of the long vacation of 1872, he was uneasy. "Remaining up here alone is not favourable to work of any kind," he decided and left for other scenes.

His fellows liked him — with reservations — and liked having a different kind of celebrity in their midst. Though he often amused, he sometimes disturbed them. He could enliven with jokes and gravely spoken absurdities, but his quick intelligence was critical. He was too insistently clever sometimes, and he would seize on and hold up the stupidities in a situation or someone else's conversation rather uncomfortably. At least one of his colleagues thought he was insolent. Another reported that Dodgson was "oppressed by a sense of gravity," for Carroll's moods were subject to sudden change, and the jester might suddenly become morose and silent.

The academic community affords the stimulating society

111

of intellectual people. Its stock in trade is pure thought, which comes out impurely but often entertainingly in incessant conversation. It is an exciting if rather bloodless atmosphere, and Dodgson both helped create it and breathed it all the time.

There was a disputativeness about Charles Dodgson, a wish to argue and a desire to win the argument, whether about a point in mathematics, where he was an acknowledged and very articulate authority, or about university affairs, where he was not an authority but was equally articulate. He was not always friendly or kind in his attitude toward his associates. Frigidity as well as warmth was part of his nature, and his fellows were not shown the almost helpless affection he reserved for appealing small girls.

Charles Lutwidge Dodgson was a celibate member of a monastic society associating with men of ideas. It is a tight little world in which petty subjects loom large. There is a continual struggling for recognition and preferment. Disputes are numerous and factions deadly. Knock-down-and-drag-out pugnacity is not countenanced, but there is inevitably a kind of tit-for-tat, slap-for-slap warfare that is as continual as it is discreet. Noble-minded as they may be about their own subjects, scholars are seldom noble-minded about their university interests, and Dodgson was no different. By temperament he was the complete don.

He could not, like Tennyson, mow his own lawn at Farringford or tend his own garden anywhere. He lived in college rooms waited on by college servants. He had neither wife nor children. He was an onlooker, the spectator at a remove from life. The women he knew and liked were the wives of other men. He enjoyed the children — if they were girls — of other people. There was not the blood and muscle of actuality in the central part of his life.

112

Probably Lewis Carroll could not have lived easily with too much of the actual. His temperament was that of the critical spectator. Perhaps he hung back from trial of what he knew instinctively he was not mentally and emotionally equipped to cope with. This does not mean that he did not feel the lack of the things he did not have or that he did not struggle to fill the voids of which he was sometimes painfully aware.

His writings, his reading, his picture taking, and his mathematics were not enough. His eighteen-mile walks were not long enough. He had to fill all of his waking hours with diversion and distraction. Would you like to win every race at the track? Charles Dodgson could tell you how. He explained his system of betting, using the Derby odds to prove his point, in a letter to *Bell's Life in London and Sporting Chronicle* early in his career as a mathematical lecturer. Years later he expatiated in complicated detail on his system in the *Pall Mall Gazette*. The Reverend C. L. Dodgson was probably never at a race track in his life, but the mathematical laws of chance and probability were his business.

Like the White Knight, he concocted dozens of ingenious inventions and devised a series of complicated parlor games. He had already advised the post office how better to manage its affairs and Covent Garden how to regulate its traffic. His mind would not be still. Some of the employments he found for it seem the almost desperate makeshift of a solitary man who had to do almost anything to fill in his time. The very number and diversity of the occupations he had to create for himself as he grew older make it obvious that he must sometimes have suffered black-pit loneliness.

For eighteen years William Ewart Gladstone had represented Oxford University in Parliament. In 1865, after a week of voting, Gladstone was defeated, and the seat went to a rival. Dodgson burlesques the contest in an anonymous pamphlet which described it in mathematical fashion. "The Dynamics of a Parti-cle" may have been uproariously funny at a time when the public knew to whom and to what his symbols referred. It is unintelligible now.

In the same year Dodgson printed and distributed another pseudomathematical treatise, "The New Method of Evaluation as applied to *pi*." This dealt with the dispute over the Regius Professorship of Greek. Using their initial letters to designate the university, the language, the professor, and the professorship, Dodgson reduced his equation to the lowest terms and called the result J, for Benjamin Jowett, whose advanced theological opinions he deplored. Dodgson's pamphlets were unsigned but all Oxford knew him their author. People bought and applauded.

Thus encouraged, Dodgson responded with more humorous diatribes against changes proposed by various university bodies. Proposals were made to add to the laboratory accommodations of the department of physics and to convert The Parks into a cricket ground. Dodgson was against both proposals and in "Facts, Figures, and Fancies" attacked them both. He defended The Parks in a parody of Goldsmith's "Deserted Village."

> Ill fares the place, to luxury a prey,
> Where wealth accumulates, and minds decay . . .

Dodgson's wrath was really kindled when Dean Liddell, a "building dean," made changes at his beloved Christ Church. All his wrath poured out in *The New Belfry of Christ Church, Oxford, A Monograph by D.C.L.*, published by James Parker and Co., 1872. Dodgson meant this one bitterly. Under his scrambled initials on the title page he placed the line from Keats's "Endymion," "A thing of beauty is a joy for ever," and under that a hollow square captioned, "East view of the new Belfry, Ch. Ch., as seen from the Meadows." In thirteen brief chapters, Dodgson described the new belfry, its perpetrators, its appearance, and what he thought of all three.

In 1871 one of the old canon's houses between the cathedral and Tom Quad had been razed so that there could be a direct approach from the Quad to the church. At the same time, Dean Liddell had the bells moved from the cathedral tower to a new belfry over the stairs into the Great Hall. It was change, and Dodgson was affronted. In his thirteen chapters, as barbed as they were brief, the delicate satirist of the *Alice* books managed to call the new belfry: a meat-safe, a box, a Greek Lexicon, a parallelopiped, a bathing-machine, a bar of soap, a tea chest, and a clothes-horse. It sounds very much as if Dodgson did not like the belfry. It is also plain that, at this time anyway, Dodgson did not like either Dean Liddell or his architect. In his first chapter Dodgson gave this as the origin of the belfry's design:

> The head of the House, and the architect, feeling a natural wish that their names should be embodied, in some conspicuous way, among the alterations then in progress, conceived the beautiful and unique idea of representing, by means of a new Belfry, a gigantic copy of a Greek Lexicon. But, before the idea had been reduced to a working form, business took them both to London for a few days, and during their absence, somehow (*this* part of the busi-

ness has never been satisfactorily explained) the whole thing was put into the hands of a wandering architect, who gave the name of Jeeby. As the poor man is now incarcerated at Hanwell, we will not be too hard upon his memory, but will only say that he professed to have originated the idea in a moment of inspiration, when idly contemplating one of those high colored, and mysteriously decorated chests which, filled with dried leaves from gooseberry bushes and quickset hedges, profess to supply the market with tea of genuine Chinese growth.

So the Greek lexicon, which was to memorialize Dean Liddell's chief literary effort, became an imitation tea chest instead. Oxford laughed with Dodgson and *The New Belfry* went quickly through five editions.

More changes were made at Christ Church. Dodgson dashed off and sold more pamphlets: "Objections submitted to the Governing Body of Christ Church, Oxford, against certain proposed alterations in the Great Quadrangle"; "The Vision of the Three T's"; "The Blank Cheque." All of his Oxford effusions he brought together in *Notes by an Oxford Chiel*, issued by Parker in Oxford in 1874. Topical and possibly amusing at the time, the book is dull and only partially intelligible now. Dodgson was a nimble-witted jester in his nonsense fantasies, but heavy-witted when he danced flat-footedly about the throne of the deanery, indignant about Oxford matters.

In 1872 Dodgson partly assuaged his loneliness by obtaining an articulate skeleton from Professor Barclay Thompson. He did not buy the skeleton for actual companionship but in renewed pursuit of his medical studies.

There was a parade of small girls with their mothers or governesses to his rooms to be given cakes and tea and to have their pictures taken. One of his new toys was a mechanical bat. On one occasion it flew out the window and landed on the loaded tray a college servitor was carrying across Tom Quad. The startled waiter dropped his tray and everything on it with a smash and clatter which must have overjoyed Dodgson's small guests.

He was not, of course, always in Oxford. He was in London, in Guildford with his sisters, and during the long vacation, at the seashore where he went every summer for fifteen or twenty years. The journeys were not long, for England is not large, but Dodgson packed and prepared each time with all the forethought and care a less precise person might expend on a world tour. He wrapped his clothing and every article he was taking with him separately in paper so that, as Collingwood says, his trunks and bags contained almost as much paper as content. He counted out his money into different purses and into separate compartments of each purse so that he would have the exact sum ready for his tickets and the exact change for tips or for newspapers, periodicals, books, and the like that he might purchase on his journey. He was beginning to develop the mannerisms and eccentricities for which many of his contemporaries remembered him.

One thing he carried with him always on his journeys. This was the small black bag containing games, puzzles, and copies of the two *Alice* books for any small girls he might be able to meet on the trains, in omnibuses, on the beach — anywhere. He sought them out wherever he went. His hunger to expend and receive love seemed to gnaw at him. He could not satisfy it in the normal circumstances of his life. He expressed it, almost desperately sometimes, to the little girls he met.

He had made many child friends at Margate, where in

1870 he spent five weeks at the shore with his sisters. He found the parents of some of them pleasant too, but "very few turned out to be above the commercial class." The snob in Dodgson did not like that. He was much happier in January 1873 as a guest at Hatfield, the ancestral home of Oxford's Lord Chancellor, hobnobbing with Lord Salisbury and Lord Eustace Cecil. The three men inspected the restoration at St. Alban's Cathedral, then walked the five miles back to Hatfield for an evening of dancing, conjuring, and storytelling. Dodgson told more than a hundred children there part of the new children's story he was already writing, *Sylvie and Bruno*. The next day he told them another chapter of the tale. Soon afterward he was in London to try another cure for his stammering.

"A working life is a happy one," Dodgson wrote in his diary, "but oh that mine were better and nearer to God!" By his own choice, he never went further in the Church than his deaconship. The stammering was one handicap. There were other obstacles, deep in the nervousness and the warring elements in his nature that produced the stammer. He could not resolve the inner conflicts signalized by his stammer no matter how much work of how many kinds he burdened himself with, but there was no stammer when he talked with children. He was at ease. There was no conflict.

All this is not a picture of a very happy man. Dodgson was an eminently successful writer. He was a valued member of an exclusive academic society. He was a celebrated amateur photographer. He was a respected mathematician. He had the money to indulge his passion for the theater, to entertain, to disport himself socially as much as he pleased. Yet there is no mistaking the dissatisfaction he felt. The humorist, as Lear, is often depressed. The wit is not always a happy man. There seems more to it than this with Dodgson.

There was a tradition in his family that Dodgson had been disappointed in love. This was the usual romantic explanation for bachelorhood or spinsterhood in Victorian times. Collingwood says outright: "One cannot read this little volume [Dodgson's posthumous verse] without feeling that the shadow of some disappointment lay over Lewis Carroll's life. Such I believe to have been the case . . ." Derek Hudson in *Lewis Carroll* (1954), the most sensible and intelligent of twentieth-century biographies of Dodgson, says that Collingwood was referring to Carroll's love for Ellen Terry.

Dodgson, who had seen and adored Ellen Terry on the stage in 1856 when she was a child of eight, did not meet her until she was nearly seventeen and already married to George Frederick Watts, who had painted her portrait. Dodgson watched for her every appearance on the stage, pursued the meeting, and became the intimate not only of the young actress who fascinated him but of all the Terry family. He saw Ellen Terry often in 1866, and they became close friends.

Ellen Terry's first marriage lasted only two years. It ended by her eloping with E. W. Godwin and exiling herself from stage and friends in Hertfordshire, where her two children were born. As soon as she returned to society and the stage, her Olivia, then her Portia brought her great acclaim. She became Henry Irving's leading lady at the Lyceum. Dodgson, who had seen her in *The Wandering Heir*, her first performance after her return, sought her out again. He saw her in every new role. Ellen Terry soon married Charles Kelly, but Dodgson persisted. The close friendship between the famous actress, who became Dame Ellen Terry and lived until 1928, and the author of *Alice in Wonderland* lasted all his life.

It has been conjectured also that Dodgson was in love with Alice Liddell. Perhaps Mrs. Liddell's dislike of Dodgson was based partly on objections to him as an unsuitable suitor, some one she did not wish to have too much about the deanery as Alice grew up. The thesis of *The White Knight*, by Alexander Taylor (1952), is that Dodgson was in love with Alice.

It is very possible that Dodgson was in love with Ellen Terry. Many men were. It is unlikely, as Hudson points out, that the love could have led to marriage or that Ellen Terry felt more than a deep affection for Lewis Carroll. It is obvious to anyone who ever read the *Alice* books that he was in love with Alice Liddell. He practically avows his love in his dedicatory verses, and the books in their entirety are expressions of his love for the child and then the young girl. This does not mean that Dodgson ever contemplated marriage with Alice Liddell or that he ever intimated to her or to her family that he wished to marry her. Alice Liddell, who as Alice Hargreaves wrote tenderly about Lewis Carroll in her later life, never suggested that he did.

It is highly probable that Lewis Carroll was in love with many of his small girl friends. Many things can be meant by the phrase "in love." As many men are, Dodgson was dependent on feminine society, even if he preferred it to be that given him by very young girls. With his love of his own childhood and his generalized love of all childhood, he could share with them more than he could share with grown women. Whether he recognized it or not, he probably knew

120

some ecstasy in his love for Ellen Terry, Alice Liddell, Xie Kitchin, Gertrude Chataway, and some of the others. He could feel gentle, tender, and protective with them. He could show off before them without fear of derision, even his own. He reacted to their affection and admiration and wrote better than he knew. He warmed to the physical beauty of small girls, to their trust, and to their innocence. He loved them.

It went that far. It is doubtful that Dodgson could have let his emotions go further.

In this respect Charles Dodgson was not unique. The fastidious bachelor, witty, charming, a little eccentric perhaps but elegant and often physically attractive, is a familiar figure on many college and university faculties. Often he lives in a dormitory suite or in tastefully furnished and precisely kept quarters on or just off the college grounds. Charles Dodgson is the prototype of these men who are attracted by the intellectual life and feel safe in a rarefied atmosphere where their talents, usually critical, can be appreciated; of these men who are often a little feminine in character without being in the least effeminate.

Often, as Dodgson did with earned right, they feel a little superior to the world about them, even to the tight little world they have chosen. Instinctively they are spectators rather than participants, more at home in the culture of the past than in the welter of the present. Though they may not acknowledge the truth to others or to themselves, they know that they are not equipped to compete in coarser enterprises or surroundings, and that they would dislike activities which might offend their sensitivities or their sense of the niceties. They are a little timid perhaps, with an aloofness of manner that safeguards them against the accusation. They would rather suffer the pangs of unrequited love occasionally than risk the realities of its being requited.

With Dodgson the difference was that he was Lewis Carroll. He had more life in him than most men. The artist usually has. Denied expression of it in the usual ways afforded the run of men, he sought it in words, photography, religion, words, long walks, inventions, the theater, words, mathematics — and words again, always in written words.

Some of the words were not words that everyone knows, or knew before he found them.

He was at the family home in Guildford and had gone for a walk alone one bright summer day, "when suddenly there came into my head one line of verse — one solitary line — 'For the Snark *was* a Boojum, you see.' I knew not what it meant, then: I know not what it means, now; but I wrote it down: and sometime afterwards, the rest of the stanza occurred to me, that being its last line: and so by degrees, at odd moments during the next year or two, the rest of the poem pieced itself together, that being its last stanza."

The poem was *The Hunting of the Snark*, weirdest and most grotesque of all Lewis Carroll's drolleries.

Henry Holiday, a London painter and designer of stained glass, came to Oxford to paint a frieze in one of the college chapels. Dodgson met him, and Holiday gave him a series of drawings he had done of nude children. Dodgson was intrigued by them and decided to make similar studies of nude children with his camera. That was the beginning of his relationship with the painter and sculptor. He then asked Holiday if he could draw grotesques and gave him the first three "fits" of the *Snark* to see if he could make suitable illustrations for the poem.

Ruskin, whom he asked to his rooms, to inspect Holiday's sketches, discouraged him. He did not think Holiday could illustrate the book satisfactorily. Ruskin was wrong. Trusting to his own judgment, Dodgson sent the first three fits to Macmillan, November 5, 1875. He wrote the other four the next day, and Holiday went ahead with his drawings. Dodgson wanted the poem out in time for sale at Christmas of that year, but the publisher could not make this deadline. Dodgson rewrote and reworked his verse, and *The Hunting of the Snark*, "An Agony in Eight Fits," was published just before Easter in late March of 1876.

Dodgson began his preface with,

> If — and the thing is wildly possible — the charge of writing nonsense were ever brought against the author of this brief but instructive poem . . .

In their *Handbook of the Literature of the Rev. C. L. Dodgson*, Sidney Williams and Falconer Madan, with great restraint, describe the *Snark* as "the impossible voyage of an improbable crew to find an inconceivable creature." Edward Lear had written of an owl and a pussy cat sailing to sea in a pea-green boat. Arithmetically, Dodgson went Lear many times better. In a boat whose bowsprit often got mixed up with its rudder he launched a Bellman, a Boots, a maker of Bonnets and Hoods, a Barrister, a Broker, a Billiard-marker, a Banker, a Beaver, a Baker, a Butcher. All of them were after a Snark who turned out to be a Boojum.

People have been trying to find abstruse meanings in the *Snark* or reading them into it ever since. Dodgson never tried. He admitted that the poem bore some relationship to the "Jabberwocky" in the *Looking-Glass* and explained one or two of his "portmanteau" words. These words he con-

123

cocted from combining other words, as "frumious" for "fuming" and "furious." "Snark" was perhaps "snake" and "shark." He had no explanation for the verse tale itself. All he knew was that the Snark was really a Boojum.

That, he told inquirers, was exactly what he meant and nothing more. Again and again he told people he knew of no other meaning for his poem. Twenty years after it had been published, he wrote a group of children this answer to their question: "As to the meaning of the *Snark?* I'm very much afraid I didn't mean anything but nonsense! Still, you know, words mean more than we mean to express when we use them: so a whole book ought to mean a great deal more than what the writer meant. So, whatever good meanings are in the book, I'm very glad to accept as the meaning of the book."

All of them after a Snark who turned out to be a Boojum

Nine

Among all the quivering contradictions hidden by the sedate clerical exterior of the Reverend C. L. Dodgson was this: He was a salesman. He had valuable properties to sell. He knew it, and he made sure they were sold. In today's parlance, he was a promoter and a relentless merchandiser.

As routine, his publishers sent out copies of his books for review. In addition, Dodgson sent presentation copies in bulk, some to friends but many to important and influential people. He spent an entire day at Macmillan's in 1876 inscribing eighty presentation copies of the *Snark*. He was continually checking with his publisher by letter or visit on the sale of his books. He picked his illustrators not only for the artistic value of their work, but also for the possible influence of their work on sales. If he paid John Tenniel 148 pounds for forty-two illustrations for *Alice in Wonderland* and rather more for the fifty in the *Looking-Glass*, as well as the 203 pounds and 16 shillings he paid the engravers, he wanted his money's worth.

Dodgson detested and fought the system whereby the bookseller makes larger profits on the sale of a book than either author or publisher. He kept advocating cheaper editions of *Alice* and the *Looking-Glass* so as to bring them within purchase range of a larger part of the public. He devised and sold an *Alice* stamp case decorated with pictures of the Cheshire Cat and the Duchess's baby turning into a pig. With the case he sold a small booklet, "Eight or Nine Wise Words on Letter-Writing." He even circularized his friends for the names of booksellers and stationers who might be persuaded to stock and sell the item.

Years after original publication of the book, Dodgson shortened and simplified the story, had some of the illustrations enlarged, and marketed a *Nursery Alice* for children aged "from nought to five." More than twenty years after the publication of *Alice's Adventures in Wonderland*, when more than 120,000 copies of the two *Alice* books had already been sold, he borrowed back the manuscript of *Alice's Adventures Under Ground* which he had lettered and illustrated for Alice Liddell, had it reproduced, and placed the facsimile on the market. The profits from this enterprise — for Dodgson was generous as well as businesslike — went to children's homes and hospitals, but the venture served to increase further the sale of all his children's books.

Dodgson had long planned another children's story and was determined this time to strike out on a new line, just as he had struck out on a new and original line when he sent his heroine underground and through a looking-glass. He was keeping records, as he kept intricate and unending records of so many things, of the amusing sayings of children. He had already told some of his new stories at Lord Salisbury's and published some of them in magazines. As always, this was only one of his tasks.

He was writing against vivisection and against the admission of women students to Oxford. He was inventing word games and puzzles. He was working on more of his mathematical disquisitions, and making new child friends everywhere he could.

The seaside was his best hunting ground for this. When he saw a pretty small girl with sand pail and shovel on the beach or wading in the water, he managed to make friends with her and to meet her parents, obtain their consent, and turn the acquaintanceship into an uncle-child intimacy deepened by the fact that he was Lewis Carroll. Though he was apt to deny the Carroll identity in Oxford, he exploited it in his search for affection.

After one seaside vacation he returned to Guildford and recorded his 1877 conquests, exulting that he had more child friends than in any previous year. He listed them: Minnie, Loui, Edith, Annie, and Lucy Waddy; Margie, Ruth, Dora, Helen, and Maude Dymes; Dora Christie . . . He added the names of seventeen other children whom he had got to know but not, he said, as close friends. More lists followed at later dates.

Dodgson was in London for *New Men and Old Acres* at the Court. Tom Taylor was part-author of the day, and Ellen Terry was in it. In 1877 he delighted in the child acting in *Goody Two-Shoes* and decided that Carrie Coote, a girl of about eight, would be just the child for *Alice* when it was staged. The acting of children fascinated him. Usually he went backstage after the performance and presented copies of the *Alice* books to the players.

He was photographing Ellen Terry and her sister, Kate. He was photographing other celebrities, but mostly photographing children and now, when he could, in the nude.

The Greeks considered the human body beautiful and so portrayed it in their sculpture. For centuries the nude had been a subject for painters. Prudish as they often were, educated Victorians had no objection to the nude in art, and there were other photographers besides Dodgson who found nude small children the ultimate subject for portrait photography. Dodgson was an artist. Beauty of line and form appealed to him. He had seen Holiday's studies of naked children. He wrote Harry Furniss, illustrator of his later children's books, that he wished the illustrations of the children in the story could be in the nude but that "some *Mothers* are awfully particular."

As early as 1867 he was trying nude photographs of a child whose mother brought her to his studio. He took photographs of other children "mostly in their favorite state of 'nothing to wear.'" Always they were little girls. "Naked children are so perfectly pure and lovely," he wrote. He did not mean small boys: "They always seem to need clothes — whereas one hardly sees why the lovely forms of girls should *ever* be covered up."

Dodgson was punctilious about obtaining permission for his nude studies and refrained if his small subject showed the slightest self-consciousness, but, again as always, he was intent on his objective when there was something he wanted. In the late 1870 he had a young woman artist he

129

had met bring a small model from London and did six nude pictures of her. Two weeks later he feared that two small girls, brought to his rooms by their mother, would be too nervous even to take off their shoes and stockings. He was surprised and pleased "to find they were ready for any amount of undress and seemed delighted at being allowed to run about naked."

He proposed to Mrs. Chataway that he pose little Gertrude Chataway, to whom he had dedicated the *Snark* in an acrostic poem, in the nude. Evidently permission was not granted.

All mothers of small girls he knew and wished to pose nude were not enthusiastic. Innocent as Dodgson's conscious intent may have been, they could place their own construction on it. The nude in art was one thing. An unmarried don of Christ Church in his middle forties posing their girls naked in his rooms was another, they felt. A genteel malevolence is the conversational rule in the sheltered precincts of academe at any time. Gossip thrives in all college communities. Undoubtedly there was gossip about the newest of the Reverend C. L. Dodgson's eccentricities. Undoubtedly it was sharply suggestive, and undoubtedly Dodgson heard it. In 1880, after having taken pictures for twenty-four years and for long periods almost living for his photography, he gave it up completely.

He had given up his principal avocation. A year later, 1881, he gave up his profession and resigned as mathematical lecturer at Christ Church, retiring from active teaching after a career of twenty-five years.

Dodgson had never liked lecturing and he had always had a low opinion of the intelligence of his undergraduates. In resigning, he wrote Dean Liddell that he wanted to have

130

his time free for writing, "partly in the cause of Mathematical education, partly in the cause of innocent recreation for children, and partly, I hope . . . in the cause of religious thought."

At forty-nine years of age he was glad to be rid of one of his duller chores. He could remain in residence at Christ Church and perform such other duties for the college as he wished. Yet he knew a momentary reluctance when he delivered his last lecture on November 30, 1881 to an audience of exactly two undergraduates. "There is a sadness in coming to the end of anything in life. Man's instincts cling to the Life that will never end."

It was hardly the end of anything for the endlessly occupied Charles Dodgson. He had scores of projects outlined on paper or in his mind. He believed it was impossible to attempt too much if you really liked what you were doing. "I appeal to anyone who has ever worked *con amore* at any subject whatever," he wrote in the *St. James's Gazette*, "to support me in asserting that, when you really love the subject you are working at, the 'physical strain' is absolutely *nil* . . ."

Dodgson lengthened his afternoon walks. One day he walked twenty-seven miles. He worked at his correspondence. In 1861 he had begun to make brief extracts of every letter he received or wrote, cross-referencing them in a notebook which by the time he died contained 98,721 entries. He kept his papers in green cardboard boxes on a revolving stand. Everything had to be in precise order. He rose early, went to chapel, worked in the morning and at night, walked in the afternoon, either alone, with a fellow don, or with some child friend through The Parks or the Christ Church Meadows.

One day in June of 1882 he tried out a velocipede, rode it for four miles, and evidently rode on occasion thereafter. He published a song, "Dreamland." He invented still another new game, "Misch-Masch," wrote a paper on a new method of judging tennis tournaments, and another on the rules for reckoning postage. Dodgson advocated double postage on Sundays and a new money-order form. Good, bad, and indifferent — a lot of it very indifferent — the work poured from his pen.

Much of his correspondence was to and from small girls. His letters of this kind are far from indifferent. They are warm with affection, alive with fancy, tender, sentimental, and sometimes awkwardly kittenish.

Usually his letters to children were short notes on half-sheets of notepaper in the purple ink that he liked. Many of them were decorated with sketches. Sometimes he made puzzles of these letters by substituting pictures for words. Most of the letters he signed "your loving friend, C. L. Dodgson," but there was no pretense that he was not Lewis Carroll. Sometimes he referred playfully to something his friend Lewis Carroll had said. Sometimes he signed a letter with both his names. Sometimes he wrote to say why he could not write.

This was to Gaynor Simpson:

My name is spelt with a "G," that is to say "*Dodgson*." Anyone who spells it the same as that wretch (I mean, of course, the Chairman of Committees in the House of Commons) offends me *deeply* and *for ever!* It is a thing I *can* forget, but *never can forgive!* If you do it again, I shall call you " 'aynor." Could you live happy with such a name?

132

In 1879 he wrote Gertrude Chataway from Reading Station while waiting for a train: "As I have been here for half an hour, I have been studying Bradshaw [timetable] (most things, you know, ought to be studied; even a trunk is studded with nails) . . ."

In 1884 he wrote Beatrice Earl, daughter of Oxford's professor of Anglo-Saxon, in a very shaky hand to indicate how terribly frightened he was even to dare proposing the favor he asked: "I want to borrow (I can scarcely muster courage to say it!) your *eldest* sister. Oh, how the very thought of it frightens me! Do you think she would come? I don't mean alone . . ."

Usually, Dodgson would countenance only one small girl visitor at a time. Two was too many unless they behaved very, very well. The visit was for jokes and riddles, puzzles, tea with thin bread and butter in his big study. Sometimes it was chess, checkers, then some game of his own inventing. Often the visits were preceded by a walk through The Parks or about the Magdalen Walks, or a ferry trip to Marston Fields.

Julia and Ethel Arnold, granddaughters of Dr. Thomas Arnold, were for a time favorite companions. Dodgson refused to go to their house for Ethel. He had tried it once, and her dachshund had bitten him. After that they met just inside The Parks. Julia, who became Mrs. Leonard Huxley, and another Arnold granddaughter, Mary, who became the celebrated novelist Mrs. Humphrey Ward, remained his friends through life. So did Alice Liddell (whom Dodgson addressed properly as Mrs. Hargreaves after her marriage in 1880), Gertrude Chataway, and the child actress Isa Bowman, who played *Alice* on the stage.

Most of his small girl friends Dodgson dropped sharply

as they began to grow up. They no longer interested him, or else he felt his motives might be suspect. "About nine out of ten, I think, of my child-friendships," he wrote, "got shipwrecked at the crucial point, 'where the stream and river meet,' and the child-friends, once so affectionate, became uninteresting acquaintances, whom I have no wish to set eyes on again."

At another time he said that the girl child usually became so different after she had grown up that the loving intimacy became merely a smile and bow when they met. Sometimes, when a coolness had developed, no one smiled and no one bowed.

Lewis Carroll had literally hundreds of warm friendships with small girls and only a few survived, but while they lasted they were a source of necessary and intense pleasure to him and to the little girls, many of whom looked back with fond reminiscence on his kindness. It was always Dodgson's kindness and gentleness they remembered. They could see through even his pretended ferocity.

Every year now Dodgson went for weeks of the summer to Eastbourne, a popular seaside resort at the south end of the South Downs, about three miles from Beachy Head in Sussex. One of the many children with whom he made friends on the sands there was Agnes Hull, daughter of a London barrister. He wrote her from Christ Church, April 30, 1881:

Hateful Spider,
(You are quite right. It doesn't *matter* a bit how one begins a letter, nor, for the matter of that, how one goes on with it, or even how one ends it — and it comes awfully easy, after a bit, to write coldly —

easier, if possible, than to write warmly. For instance, I have been writing to the Dean, on College business, and began the letter "Obscure Animalcule," and he is foolish enough to pretend to be angry about it, and to say it wasn't a proper style, and that he will propose to the Vice-Chancellor to expel me from the University: and it is all your fault!)

A little arch, perhaps, but there is the true Carrollian touch about that letter and even more to the simple postscript he added to a letter to Maud Standen: "Love to any lovable animals you may happen to have in the house."

Carroll did not send his love to little boys. Once a friend to whom he had sent a copy of one of his children's books wrote that he would like to bring his small son to meet him. Dodgson posted back a horrified *No!* He wrote in his diary: "He thought I doted on *all* children. But I'm not omnivorous! — like a pig. I pick and choose."

When a colleague tried to introduce a small boy to him in his entry in Tom Quad, Dodgson said, "I don't like little boys," went into his rooms, and closed the door. He admitted that he was fond of children, except boys. He said that to him boys were not an attractive race of beings.

He not only liked small girls, he also liked to kiss them, and he did. One day in 1880 he brought a small boy and a girl to wait in his rooms for their father, his friend Owen. When they left, Dodgson kissed the girl, whom he thought to be about fourteen. She was seventeen. Dodgson was appalled and wrote the mother a mock apology promising to kiss Hatty Owen no more. Like Queen Victoria on another occasion, Mrs. Owen was not amused. She replied frigidly that she would take care the incident was not repeated. The

casual kiss of today was not taken as casually in prudish mid-Victorian England.

Dodgson was greatly upset. He conferred with Xie's father, Dr. George Kitchin, about what notice he should take of the rebuke, then asked Owen for an explanation. He felt hurt. He knew he had done nothing wrong. He felt as put-upon as any small boy unjustly punished when he has committed no offense. After that he was careful to find out the ages of his small friends before he kissed them, and to make sure he had parental permission in advance.

There is something very pathetic about the author of *Alice in Wonderland* having to go hat in hand to lesser men and women when he sought endearing expression of the only personal emotion he seemed to feel or to allow himself to feel. If anyone had earned the right to children's affection, it was he. There is something even more pathetic about the insistence of his need, which was stronger than his dread of the churlish rebuffs he suffered. Dodgson hungered for affection. Almost as much he needed expression of affection given and returned as assurance that it was there. Stiff-backed, almost priggishly self-sufficient, he was hardly the man to ask for understanding, but he was sensitive. He could not help wincing at the Victorian squeamishness of some mothers and sometimes at the thoughtless snubs of their offspring. His coldly logical mind did him little good here. He was just puzzled and hurt like anyone else, and, again like a misunderstood small boy, rebellious.

Rebelliousness was anyway a part of Dodgson's nature.

To Dodgson, boys were not an attractive race of beings.

137

He loved Oxford and Christ Church, but he rebelled against them often, and often stingingly in print. He was the prim and proper, the almost painfully devout Church of England cleric of his time, but he rebelled against his clerical associates and even his superiors who condemned the theater as wicked. He went to the theater as often as he could. He accepted the conventions to which the Victorian world paid lip service and walked circumspectly within the rule of correct social behavior laid down for his class and profession, but he was an individual. In most outward ways, Dodgson was a conformist, but he was also an individualist, a strongly marked and independent man, a logician but also a poet. Try as he might to be like everyone else, he had to be Charles Lutwidge Dodgson, who was not like anyone else.

In August 1880 he took two small girls to see an American circus in London and, with his penchant for child performers, was pleased that he could talk with two circus children, a girl of eight and another of thirteen, whom he found practicing their act with a pony. A month later he met and made friends with another American girl, Lily Alice Godfrey. In the end he was not as pleased.

He promised her a copy of the *Snark*, but was taken aback when on parting she refused to be kissed. The child explained that she never kissed gentlemen. Smarting and embarrassed, the forty-eight-year-old Dodgson commented that it pained him to see the simplicity of childhood disappear so soon. Rather vengefully he added — for he'd had about enough of this nonsense and was glad to blame the world at large, or half of it, for the stupidity which exasperated him — "I fear it is true that there are no children in America."

Ten

In December of 1882 Dodgson was elected Curator of the Common Room of Christ Church. The senior Common Room was in reality a sort of elegant club for the dons, the graduate members of The House. It was a place where they could read or write letters, order what refreshments they chose, entertain their guests, talk after dinner at the high table in the hall. The curator was, in effect, the club's president as well as its secretary and in many ways its member-steward.

Dodgson took his responsibility for the conduct of the Common Room with great seriousness. To his own satisfaction and the annoyance of his fellows, he drew up long lists of rules and regulations, most of which proved unworkable. He kept the accounts, paid the bills, oversaw the work of the servants and, with the help of a willing committee, selected the wines for the Common Room's cellar.

Dodgson went at his curatorship with all his love of detail and his punctilious gusto. He might have been attacking a new problem in logic or in calculus. He held wine-tasting luncheons at which he and his committee soberly selected the ports and sherries to be stocked and served on order. He weighed the cost of Chablis against that of Madeira and calculated the prices which should be charged Common Room imbibers. With august medical advisers he decided on the most efficacious and painless way of disposing of the club's overage cat.

Characteristically, Dodgson turned his stewardship to literary account. A year after taking office he printed a pamphlet, "Twelve Months in a Curatorship by One Who Has Tried It." Three years later he repeated the performance. Before he relinquished the office which he held for nearly ten years he put out "Curiosissima Curatoria." Like his earlier *Notes by an Oxford Chiel*, these pamphlets were humorous in treatment but humorless in intent.

On his fifty-first birthday Dodgson said he felt no older than he had felt at twenty-one. He was as youthful and as active as ever. The long walks continued. He bought a patent exerciser, used it, and liked it so well that he bought others and gave them to friends.

He invented a complicated memory system. He invented a method for taking notes in the dark. As he had written Dean Liddell that he planned, he was working in mathematics, at his stories for children, and at religious duties. Perhaps because he was jealous of his time, perhaps because he felt he had won the right to do more and more as he pleased, he began to cultivate some of the eccentricities that marked his later years.

140

He ceased much of his dining out. He pointedly refused invitations to social events but as pointedly appeared when he had not been formally invited. He came, he said, because he had *not* been invited. His friends merely let it be known that they would be at home on given dates and left acceptance or refusal of invitations that were implied but carefully not stated up to him.

If he did appear and heard or overheard a remark which in some way affronted him, Dodgson simply turned and left. Usually he was on all his dignity, but one Christ Church man, hearing odd noises from under a table in a house he was visiting, poked his head beneath it and met the eyes of the Reverend C. L. Dodgson just a few inches away. Dodgson had submerged to play with the host's children.

The young man who had been an undiscourageable lion-hunter became in middle age a very reluctant lion himself. He refused to read reviews of his books or press comments about their author. For fear they were seeking his autograph, he would not answer letters from people he did not know. He would either not answer at all or get a friend to answer and sign the letter "Lewis Carroll."

Letters addressed to him as "Carroll" infuriated him. He was the Reverend Charles Lutwidge Dodgson and angrily declared that he was. If anyone attempted reference to the *Alice* books in his presence, he fled. Dodgson in these days was making concessions to no one. The man who delighted in picking flaws in the reasoning of others was beautifully inconsistent and gloriously unreasonable. In May 1888 he bought a Hammond typewriter, and a friend showed him how to use it. Now he could safely answer letters without fear of anyone he did not wish to have it getting either his autograph or a sample of his writing.

Dodgson enjoyed his typewriter. The archconservative loved novelties. Inventive himself, he enthused over inventions. He was quick to purchase an early camera, then others as improved cameras were developed. He utilized the typewriter as soon as he could. In 1890 he went to hear a phonograph and was delighted. "It is a pity that we are not fifty years further on in the world's history, so as to get this wonderful invention in its *perfect* form. It is now in its infancy — the new wonder of the day, just as I remember Photography was about 1850." Were he alive, Dodgson would revel in today's electronic and audiovisual equipment.

At the same time that he was being coyly reclusive, Dodgson was being happy and expansive in acknowledging authorship of *Alice in Wonderland* when, with book by Savile Clarke, it was staged as an operetta at the Prince of Wales Theatre in London in 1886. The musical version of the two *Alice* books was staged again by Richard Mansfield at the Royal Globe, with Dodgson's child friend Isa Bowman as Alice and her sister Emsie as Dormouse and as Second Ghost, who sang and danced a sailor's hornpipe. Dodgson though them both wonderful.

With another *Alice* venture he was having trouble. After borrowing the manuscript of *Alice's Adventures Under Ground* from Mrs. Hargreaves, he took it to London to have the pages photographed and plates made for the printer. The platemaker said he would have to leave the book. This Dodgson refused to do. He had a different zincographer come to his own Oxford studio, where he took his pictures with Dodgson turning the pages.

The man sent Dodgson the first plates. Then he and the rest of the plates, for which Dodgson had paid in advance, disappeared. Months later he reappeared long enough to leave eight more plates at Macmillan's. Fourteen were still missing and so, once more, was the man. Dodgson decided to hire a detective to unearth him. He hired a solicitor instead, had a summons served, and appeared as plaintiff before a magistrate.

The defendant did not appear. The magistrate's clerk put Dodgson in the witness box and harried him with questions. As Dodgson wrote Mrs. Hargreaves, the man "seemed to think that, if he only bullied me enough, he would soon catch me out in a falsehood." The clerk didn't know his man. The gentle Lewis Carroll could be the relentless Charles L. Dodgson. This time he obtained a warrant for the zincographer's arrest so that he would have to show up for trial as a defaulter. Frightened, the man showed up the day before the scheduled trial and handed over the fourteen negatives. Seemingly he had been hiding from his creditors. Dodgson won, but he had to pay a second time to have someone else make the plates. Though severely annoyed at this and at having to make two trips back from Eastbourne to court, Dodgson was triumphant.

In 1887 Dodgson published his *Game of Logic*. Dedicated to "My Child-Friends," the book had with it a cardboard diagram in an envelope, four red counters, and four black ones. With these the players, by following his rather complicated directions, could work out problems in logic. The book has to do with propositions, syllogisms, premises, conclusions, and fallacies, but Dodgson's textual explanations are humorous. Logic and mathematics were fun for Dodgson. He assumed they were fun for his readers and did his best to present his subject through ingenious and amusing argument. He has a section on "Cross Questions" and solves them under "Crooked Answers."

Dodgson explained that the game "requires one Player *at least*. I am not aware of any game that can be played with *less* than this number; while there are several that require *more*: take Cricket, for instance, which requires twenty-two." He thought it an added advantage that besides being an endless source of amusement his *Game of Logic* provided a little instruction as well. "But is there any great harm in *that*, so long as you get plenty of amusement?"

Dodgson's comment here points one of the essential differences between his early and later writing for children. The two *Alice* books were free of conscious purpose. They came unsought, he said, into his mind, and he expressed his thoughts as they came to him. His later work was planned and had conscious purpose. His intent was didactic.

He wished to instruct. As a teacher, he wished to instruct in logic and in mathematics. As a clergyman he wished to instruct in morals and religion. *Alice's Adventures in Wonderland*, *Through the Looking-Glass*, and *The Hunting of the Snark* are as free and irresponsible as Dodgson's sense of the deliciously absurd, the vividly imagined, and the golden airiness of childhood. In contrast, his later writing for children is restricted and constricted by his desire to inculcate an awareness of serious moral values. This is particularly true of *Sylvie and Bruno* (1889), which he considered perhaps his major work for children, and of *Sylvie and Bruno Concluded*, published four years later.

As he always did, Dodgson sought an illustrator before

Tenniel wrote Dodgson: "It is a curious fact that with 'Through the Looking-Glass' the faculty of making drawings for book illustration departed from me . . ."

undertaking the actual construction of his book. This time, though his reply to Dodgson's inquiry was tactfully couched, Tenniel would have none of him. In a letter to Dodgson he wrote:

> It is a curious fact that with *Through the Looking-Glass* the faculty of making drawings for book illustration departed from me, and, notwithstanding all sorts of tempting inducements, I have done nothing in that direction since.

Dodgson then approached Harry Furniss, who accepted immediately, saying in early 1885 that he had long wanted to illustrate one of Lewis Carroll's books. Tenniel shook his head and told Furniss that Dodgson was impossible and that he would not work for him for seven weeks. He was wrong. Furniss worked with Dodgson, who was more exacting than ever, for seven years. The artist got along with the author, he admitted, by letting him think that he was "wilful and erratic, bordering on insanity."

No detail of the sketches got by Dodgson's scrutiny. When Furniss submitted his roughs, he professed himself delighted with Uggug and the Professor but horrified with the Doctor and with Eric. He didn't like the face of his heroine, Lady Muriel, and said he could never have talked to her and was sure he couldn't fall in love with her. Furniss's human characters were too tall, too old, too something or other which affronted his fastidious taste, and his picturization of Bruno was impossible.

> No, no! Please don't give us the (to my mind) very ugly, quite modern costume, which shows with

such cruel distinctness a podgy, pot-bellied (excuse the vulgarism) boy, who couldn't run a mile to save his life. I want Bruno to be *strong*, but at the same time light and active — with the figure of one of the the little acrobats one sees at the circus — not "Master Tommy," who habitually gorges himself with pudding. Also that *dress* I dislike very much. Please give him a short tunic, and *real* knickerbockers — not the tight knee-breeches they are rapidly shrinking to.

The sketches and finished pictures went back and forth, with Dodgson examining and criticizing every detail. This meant a great deal of work and trouble for the artist, but Dodgson was so pleased with the final result that besides paying Furniss generously he offered him a share of the profits from the book. He was particularly pleased that Furniss drew Sylvie from a live model. Tenniel had used no model for his Alice. When the book was published, Dodgson wrote the artist, "I am grateful; and I feel sure that if *pictures* could sell a book, *Sylvie and Bruno* would sell like wildfire."

Dedicated in an acrostic to Isa Bowman, *Sylvie and Bruno* is nearly twice as long as either of the *Alice* books, and is a much more prosaic story. In many ways, it is not a child's story at all. There is a framework of adult characters and action around it. A Victorian love affair is part of it. This is told in the first person by an older man who is suffering from a heart ailment. Often he falls asleep or into oblivion of the world around him and enters into another world. Awake, he tells the story of Lady Muriel Orme and Dr. Arthur Forrester, his physician; asleep and dreaming, he talks with the fairies Bruno and Sylvie and tells their story. Thus the narrative moves in and out of Elfland and Outland.

Carroll prefaced *Sylvie and Bruno* with a long and solemn sermon. It is really a sermon by the Reverend C. L. Dodgson. In it he said that he had written his book with two conscious purposes: the first, to strike out on yet another new path in writing for children; the second, "in the hope of supplying, for the children whom I love, some thoughts that may suit those hours of innocent merriment which are the very life of Childhood; and also, in the hope of suggesting, to them and to others, some thoughts that may prove, I would fain hope, not wholly out of harmony with the greater cadences of Life."

That far he sounds like Lewis Carroll. He soon ceased to. Later in his preface, Dodgson advocated a children's Bible, a book of selected pieces from the Bible, a collection of prose and verse passages from inspiring writers, and an edition of Shakespeare's plays for girls "with all that is unseemly on the score of reverence or decency" erased. He asked that people walk solemnly in the knowledge of imminent death. He defended the theater, stated that the true end of life was the development of character, and ended with an attack on fox hunting.

It is a strange medley, and in many ways *Sylvie and Bruno* is a strange book. It is an inextricable mixture of deadly seriousness, moral preachment, some of the worst babytalk on record in the speech of Bruno, and some of the sharpest satire, choicest humor, and cleverest nonsense doggerel that its author ever penned. In most of his other books some one element of the complex character of Charles Lutwidge Dodgson asserts itself, isolates itself from the rest of him, and gives a lighted force and unity to the

148

work. In *Sylvie and Bruno* many diverse elements of the man seem striving for expression at the same time.

Charles Dodgson knew the meaning of "misch-masch." He had used "Misch-Masch" first as the title of one of his Croft household magazines. Later he used it as the name of a game which he invented in 1882. He might have saved it for the title of this book. Yet there are strains of pure Lewis Carroll, sure, light, resilient, sometimes biting, throughout the hodgepodge of *Sylvie and Bruno.*

Who, one wonders, sat for their portraits as Lord Chancellor, Warden, the Sub-Warden and his Lady? Who were the Professor and the Other Professor? Oxford must have wondered too. Like Tenniel, Dodgson would have needed no models for his fairy children and their earthly opposite, Uggug, son of the Sub-Warden and his wife. Uggug was "a hideous fat boy, about the same age as Sylvie, with the expression of a prize-pig." Perhaps he was the Duchess's baby escaped from *Alice in Wonderland.* Perhaps he was just Dodgson's dislike of all boys.

Dodgson would have needed no model either for the mad gardener who appears and reappears throughout the story each time the narrator slips from normal consciousness into his dream world. Dodgson always had such wonderful characters on tap in his imagination. The first time he appears the gardener is singing:

> He thought he saw an Elephant,
> That practised on a fife:
> He looked again, and found it was
> A letter from his wife.
> "At length I realise," he said,
> The bitterness of life."

The thoughtful gardener has something worth while to sing every time he turns up.

> He thought he saw a Rattlesnake
> That questioned him in Greek:
> He looked again, and found it was
> The middle of Next Week.
> "The one thing I regret," he said,
> "Is that it cannot speak!"

There is vividly, almost viciously, humorous dialogue in *Sylvie and Bruno*, usually between the Sub-Warden and his distinctive wife. There is a satirical aping of the academic habit of thought and speech where the two Professors enter. There is a gracious play of fancy when Dodgson is describing events and characters in Elfland. Sylvie is all elfin grace and truth. The smaller Bruno is stalwart, honest, and grubbier. He is somewhat more of a realist than his dainty sister.

Chapter Twelve opens with the Professor and the Other Professor in conference. The two fairy children are in attendance. The Other Professor has just finished reciting a very long poem which has worn Bruno out.

> The Other Professor regarded him with some anxiety. "The smaller animal ought to go to bed *at once*," he said with an air of authority.
>
> "Why *at once*?" said the Professor.
>
> "Because he can't go at twice," said the Other Professor.
>
> The Professor gently clapped his hands. "Isn't he *wonderful!*" he said to Sylvie. "Nobody else could have thought of the reason, so quick. Why, *of*

150

course he can't go at twice! It would hurt him to be divided."

This remark woke up Bruno, suddenly and completely. "I don't want to be *divided*," he said decisively.

"It does very well on a *diagram*," said the Other Professor. "I could show you in a minute, only the chalk's a little blunt."

"Take care!" Sylvie anxiously exclaimed, as he began, rather clumsily, to point it. "You'll cut your finger off, if you hold the knife so!"

"If oo cuts it off, will oo give it to *me*, please?" Bruno thoughtfully added.

There is a good deal of Lewis Carroll in that brief passage. There is insistence on literalness in the use of the word "twice." He takes it out of colloquial context to use it mathematically. There is the gentle aping of the academic manner of thought and speech. If he could diagram the division in a classroom, the Other Professor saw no valid reason why he could not bisect Bruno in practice. There is Sylvie's feminine solicitude for the man who might cut his finger. Bruno, small enough so that he habitually says "oo" for "you," shows the bloodthirstiness of many small boys.

Could Carroll read the preceding paragraph, he would point out that "a good deal" in the opening sentence can refer properly only to a card game, and not to all card games at that. The writer should have said "much" — but how much, and who is to decide? He would also point out that in geometry "bisect" meant to divide into equal parts. Nothing had been said about dividing Bruno equally. Possibly the writer meant "by sect," meaning that Bruno should be divided into pagan and Christian. There had been an indication of the pagan in Bruno, but where had the writer seen any tendency toward Christianity in him? Possibly the writer meant something entirely different from either of these suppositions. Probably he meant nothing at all.

In characteristic mood, Carroll could be like that, which is one reason the nonsense dialogue in his books is so amusing and also perhaps the reason why all of his colleagues did not always love him dearly.

Bruno is often rather like Carroll. When the Sentinel before the Royal Kennel demands, "Give your names," Bruno instantly replies, "We'd rather not! . . . We want them ourselves."

Bruno is a reasonable man too. The Other Professor was lost. The Professor and Sylvie could not find him. Once before he had lost himself in the woods. "And couldn't he find his-self again?" said Bruno. "Why didn't he shout? He'd be sure to hear his-self, 'cause he couldn't be far off, oo know."

When, just in time for the profitable Christmas market in 1893, Dodgson published *Sylvie and Bruno Concluded*, he prefaced the sequel with another sermon.

He explained that the theory behind the whole *Sylvie and Bruno* story was to show what might happen if fairies and human beings were sometimes visible to each other. He had supposed a Human being (he capitalized the adjective) capable of various psychic states in which he had varying degrees of consciousness of the fairies, and he listed the different states of fairy-consciousness he meant. He had likewise supposed fairies capable of entering the real world and had given them varying psychic states. It is interesting to

152

see Dodgson playing with the ideas and language of the new social science of psychology in 1893, but once again the clergyman is most apparent.

Far too many sermons were expected of preachers, he wrote. The result was that many of them were poor and not worth listening to. He protested against too much ritual in church. It made worship only a form. He mentioned what he considered the irreverent treatment of holy things and scolded both the theater for its caricatures of clergymen and the Salvation Army for its coarse familiarity in treating God and religion.

The piety expressed in the preface is strongly emphasized in the book, which ends with a mawkish effusion in praise of love as the jewel of life. Bruno, like Dodgson, could be a sentimentalist on occasion. Also, like Dodgson, he had a habit of seeing things a little differently from most people.

Sylvie is giving him his lessons as the book opens. Perspicaciously, Bruno notes that he has to repeat his "muddlesome tables" in arithmetic but does not have to repeat his history lessons because "history repeats itself." Sylvie then starts his spelling lesson.

Sylvie was arranging some letters on a board — E — V — I — L. "Now, Bruno," she said, "what does *that spell?*"

Bruno looked at it, in solemn silence, for a minute. "I knows what it doesn't spell!" he said at last.

"That's no good," said Sylvie. "What *does* it spell?"

Bruno took another look at the mysterious letters. "Why, it's 'LIVE,' backwards!" he exclaimed. (I thought it was, indeed.)

"How *did* you manage to see that?" said Sylvie.

"I just twiddled my eyes," said Bruno, "and then I saw it directly."

Lewis Carroll had a way of twiddling his eyes, too, and of seeing things directly.

Eleven

The Reverend Charles Lutwidge Dodgson was not merely articulate. He was voluble. When he was not lecturing or arguing, he was writing. He was writing books or letters to his small girl friends or even an open letter to the mothers of England urging a censoring of Shakespeare for little girls.

He stood up at a high desk as he wrote, or walked up and down as he told stories or waited for the tea water to boil. His restless mind spun as his restless body moved, and it spun out words. The words sped into children's books, polemics, lectures, sermons, mathematical controversy. He hurried into print with almost all he spoke. Even at night his mind did not rest and his cleverness — cleverness often seems the word for Dodgson — was not stilled.

Between the publication of the two *Sylvie and Bruno*

books he published the second part of his *Curiosa Mathematica*. "Pillow Problems" appeared in this book. These were problems in arithmetic, algebra, geometry, trigonometry, and even transcendental probabilities which he worked out mentally while lying wakeful at night. They were exercises which he devised to free his mind, as he said, of skeptical and blasphemous thoughts. He published them to show that the "mind can be made to concentrate itself on some intellectual subject (not necessarily mathematics), and thus banish those petty troubles and vexations which most people experience, and which — unless the mind be otherwise occupied — *will* persist in invading the hours of night."

"Pillow Problems" afforded him diversion of one kind and affronted no one, but they did not feed his piety, which grew more rigid with the years, or afford him other ease. It is difficult to extract emotional warmth from arithmetic, even long division.

Dodgson's child friends, he said, made up three-quarters of his life, and by his life Dodgson meant here what anyone else usually means — his personal and meaningful life aside from his profession and mechanical diversions.

The little girls he met and talked and played with in Oxford or brought to Oxford to entertain or took down from Oxford to the theater or the circus in London or made friends with on the Eastbourne sands were what gave human quality to his otherwise rather bloodless existence. They were the wife and children he did not have, just as they were the reality which, despite its fascination for him, he could not find in all the tinsel and excitement of the theater.

Isa Bowman, who had played Alice and to whom he had dedicated *Sylvie and Bruno*, was an especial favorite. He

156

often had his dream-child and her sisters, Nellie, Maggie, and Emsie, to visit him at Oxford or at Eastbourne. Of one of Isa Bowman's visits he wrote, "When people ask me why I have never married, I tell them I have never met the young lady I could endure for a fortnight — but Isa and I got on so well together that I said I should keep her a month, the length of the honey-moon, and we didn't get tired of each other."

He wrote a long, humorous poem about Maggie Bowman and for her when she visited him in Oxford in June 1889.

> When Maggie once to Oxford came,
>   On tour as "Bootle's Baby,"
> She said, "I'll see this place of fame,
>   However dull the day be."

Man and child went into the Christ Church kitchens and watched the meringues being baked. They admired the hall, the cathedral, the Broad Walk, the Worcester Gardens, St. John's. Hand in hand they walked to the Botanical Gardens, to Magdalen. They met a bishop, to whom Dodgson explained that he was showing the self-possessed little actress the sights of Oxford town.

> "Now say what kind of place it is,"
>   The Bishop gaily cried.
> "The best place in the Provinces!"
>   That little maid replied.

In 1886 Dodgson wrote his cousin Menella Wilcox, asking if she would return him some verses he had written years before for her doll. The letter was from Eastbourne.

In it he wrote: "I'm down here all alone, but happy as a king — at least, as happy as *some* kings — at any rate, I should think I'm about as happy as King Charles the First when he was in prison."

Dodgson did not like to be alone in Oxford, Eastbourne, or anywhere else. He wrote asking little girls to come and stay with him for a day, two days, a week. He begged their parents to let them come as his guests. Some came, and both he and the fortunate children were happy. Sometimes he was sharply rebuffed.

Later in life one woman, whose letter shows the disappointment she still felt, wrote that Dodgson had again and again begged her mother for permission to take her to London or to the seaside. Permission denied. She would regret it, the woman wrote, to the end of her days. "Days of close intercourse with one who, however whimsical his mind, was one of the few genuine scholar-saints were denied me because the saint was male and I was a little girl."

Dodgson would have objected to the "saint" as impious, and it is hardly an accurate description, but other little girls were more fortunate. He was all courteous attention to his small guests. He looked after their every need and put himself out to entertain them. Whatever their age, he treated them as if they were still children of ten, and some of them were considerably older. Gertrude Chataway, to whom he had dedicated *The Snark*, was twenty-six when for four days she was Dodgson's guest at Eastbourne. Some of the older girls found it tiresome to be treated as if they were still but ten years old. Others found it charming.

Charles Lutwidge Dodgson could lead the blameless life of a clerical and snobbish don of Christ Church with no risk and little difficulty. He had to risk a little more and endure some unpleasantness when he sought to live the emotional life of Lewis Carroll. His entertaining his small feminine friends could not go unnoticed.

As his photographing of the nude had done earlier, it caused gossip, and Dodgson knew it. He was not surprised. He was less hurt than determined when one of his sisters wrote questioning the propriety of his actions. His reply was sharp and decisive.

> You and your husband have, I think, been very fortunate to know so little by experience . . . of the wicked recklessness with which people repeat things to the disadvantage of others, without a thought as to whether they have grounds for asserting what they say. I have met with a good deal of utter misrepresentation of that kind. Another result of my experience is that the opinion of 'people' in general is absolutely worthless as a test of right and wrong. The only two tests I now apply to such a question as having some particular girl-friend as a guest are, first, my own conscience . . . secondly, the parents of my friend, to settle whether I have their *full* approval. . . . You need not be shocked at my being spoken against. *Any*body, who is spoken about at all, is *sure* to be spoken against by *some*body: and any action, however innocent in itself, is liable, and not at all unlikely, to be blamed by *somebody*. If you limit your actions in life to such things that *nobody* can possibly find fault with, you will not do much . . .

If Dodgson defied the critics, it was because he had to. He knew that he had to indulge what emotions he had if he was to keep what was vital in him alive. He had to rebel against minor conventions, to contradict Victorian manners. The rebellion was instinctive. Dodgson could preach earnestly, and he did, to the college servants and to Eastbourne vacationers against yielding to temptation and in favor of duty, which he believed to be the "Stern daughter of the Voice of God," but there were moods in which he was more apt to parody Wordsworth than to parrot him.

He was as proper as most old-maidish bachelors who are also clergymen, but he was also Puck, even if he was a prim Puck. In his heart of hearts he must have known that what he did in his imaginative writing was far more important than what he accomplished as a preacher or even as a mathematician. Many men could preach. Others with the gift and trained mind could do as much as he in mathematics. Only one man could write *Alice in Wonderland* and *Through the Looking-Glass*.

Dodgson had resigned his lectureship, but it was not as easy to forswear his habit of lecturing. He still had much to say, and he found the kinds of audience that he preferred to say it to. As well as preaching, he began to give lectures in logic to classes of girls in Oxford, in Eastbourne, in Guildford, and in other centers and to read his stories to children anywhere on any occasion that offered.

He demonstrated some of his mathematical puzzles and their solutions to the smaller girls of the Girls' High School in Guildford and explained his memory system to the older girls. He told the story of "Bruno's Picnic" to a large audience in the High School of Birmingham. He gave a series of lectures on logic at the Oxford Girls' High School. One day in Worcester he spoke to an audience of about a hundred girls aged six to fourteen, telling them "Bruno's Picnic" and showing them puzzles in arithmetic on the blackboard.

That was in the afternoon. In the evening he spoke seriously to another hundred older girls in the same school. Dodgson did not report what he spoke seriously about, but said it was "an experience of the deepest interest to me."

He lectured in logic at other schools, giving each pupil, according to Collingwood, his personal attention. In 1897 he undertook a course in logic at Abbot's Hospital in Guildford. Dodgson had taken a strong stand against the admission of women to the honors schools at Oxford, but he was interested in the education of girls. He gave classes in logic at Lady Margaret and at St. Hugh's Hall, where his listeners were older girls. He had two of his nieces come to Oxford so that they could attend the Girls' High School, and looked after them and fussed over them like any kindly bachelor uncle.

His interest in girls' schools even became transatlantic. A class in the Girls' Latin School in Boston started a magazine and wrote asking if they might call it "The Jabberwock." Dodgson not only gave permission, but also wished the paper well and even defined *jabberwock* for the girls as meaning "the result of much excited discussion." With his unusual inconsistency, he spoke as Lewis Carroll and signed his letter with that name. He took the magazine's editors to task for what he considered an irreverent joke in one issue, then made amends by sending them a "Lump of Sugar" in the form of a poem called "A Lesson in Latin," which he asked them to print.

It was sent to Boston from London where he was staying, and his accompanying letter was typed. He ended it by saying, "This mode of writing is, of course, an American invention. We never invent new machinery here; but we do use, to the best of our ability, the machines you send us.

For the one I am now using, I beg you to accept my best thanks, and to believe me your sincere friend, 'Lewis Carroll.' "

This was about as far as Dodgson's approval of things American went. He did not even want his young friends to go there. When Isa and Nellie Bowman talked of a planned trip to the United States, he suggested that they had better get accustomed to crossing the Atlantic by degrees. He took them on an excursion boat from Eastbourne to Hastings, some twenty miles northeast through the English Channel. The weather was rough. The girls got violently seasick. Dodgson cheered them by saying over and over that crossing the Atlantic would be very much worse.

When he was very fortunate, Dodgson was sometimes able to combine two of his loves, that for children and that for royalty. On a later visit to Hatfield he lunched and breakfasted with the Duchess of Albany. In the afternoon — it was a Sunday — he folded a fishing boat out of paper and told some of his *Sylvie and Bruno* stories to the children: Princess Alice, the small Duke of Albany, Lady Victoria Manners, Lord Haddon, and the Honorable Mabel Palmer. Happily he listed their names and titles. In 1891, when the Duchess was visiting at the Christ Church deanery, Princess Alice and the Duke of Albany called on Dodgson in his Tom Quad rooms, where he showed them how to make paper pistols. He "marked the day with a white stone" in his diary, and after the children had left Oxford, he sent a copy of his *Nursery Alice* to Princess Alice and another book to the Duke, who wrote in his thank-you note, "Alice and I want you to love us both."

Royalty or not, Dodgson loved children, unless they were boys. He added a postscript to one of his child letters:

"My best love to yourself — to your Mother my kindest regards — to your small, fat, impertinent, ignorant brother my hatred. I think that is all." He wrote it facetiously, of course, but he wrote it.

Dodgson had only himself to blame for one incident which occurred when he was trying, as he always tried, to make friends with a little girl on a train. This time the small girl who had attracted his attention was reading *Alice in Wonderland*. When she put it down, he began asking her about the book.

The mother broke in: "Isn't it sad about poor Mr. Lewis Carroll? He's gone mad, you know."

Dodgson told her he didn't know.

"Oh, I assure you it is quite true."

Dodgson, who probably did not believe the truth of the report, sent the little girl an inscribed copy of *Through the Looking-Glass*.

At the seashore, Dodgson always carried a supply of safety pins. He would present one gravely to any small girl who he saw wanted to wade but was afraid of getting her skirts wet. He believed in pins. He sent a little girl a pincushion with a picture of Interlaken on it, and his letter described the advantage of having a pin handy when you really needed one.

> For instance, you go into a shop, and you say to the man, "I want the largest penny bun you can let me have for a halfpenny." And perhaps the man looks stupid and doesn't quite understand what you mean. Then how convenient it is to have a pin ready to stick into the back of his hand, while you say, "Now then! Look sharp, stupid!"

Except that Dodgson says "you" for "oo," it might have been Bruno talking.

Dodgson stayed young in heart, young in mind, and young in body. He took care of himself. He dreaded infection and once published a pamphlet on the common cold. When Isa and Nellie Bowman were visiting him at Eastbourne and the news came that their youngest sister, Emsie, had scarlet fever, Dodgson would not even let them touch letters from home. From the other end of the room he held the letters up for them to read as best they could. He studied his medical books. He took his twenty-mile walks. He was well, and, as he admitted in one of his letters, his life was singularly free of pain or troubles. He supposed he was happy, though in another letter he advised against anyone's thinking of being either happy or unhappy.

He knew that his own happiness depended on his being busy, and he was unremittingly busy. He had a strong fear that he might not accomplish all the tasks he had set for himself. He was well and strong. He felt no diminution of his powers. He felt, in fact, that he had never thought more clearly or been able to express himself more surely. Yet it disturbed him that many of his older colleagues, even Canon Liddon, with whom he had traveled to Russia, had died and that others of his one-time associates were inactive. Dean Liddell had resigned in 1891, and the change had upset him even though Liddell was succeeded by Dodgson's close friend, Dean Paget.

"It is getting increasingly difficult," Dodgson wrote one of his sisters in 1896, "now to remember *which* of one's friends . . . have gone . . . Also, such news comes less and less as a shock, and more and more one realizes that it is an experience each of *us* has to face before long." In the same letter he said he was rising early and was often at work on the second part of his *Symbolic Logic* by seven o'clock, working an hour and a half before breakfast. He had the plan of the rest of the book in his head, and the actual writing should take him only three or four months.

He had published Part I of his *Symbolic Logic* in 1896 and was driving to finish what he considered would be his *magnum opus* in the field, but *Symbolic Logic* or no logic at all, he would not miss one event in the spring of 1897.

The Prince of Wales came to Oxford to open the Town Hall. Dodgson invited some twenty of his friends, including nearly all of the children in Christ Church, to come up to his room to watch the procession from the college roof. That night there was a formal dinner party in the Great Hall. The Prince sat on Dean Paget's right and Lord Salisbury, Chancellor of the University, on his left. Dodgson himself sat happily almost directly across the table from the Prince.

Dodgson spent the long vacation of that summer of 1897 in Eastbourne, working on his book, taking long walks — some as far as Hastings, which William the Conqueror had made famous in 1066 — and lecturing and telling his stories in the Eastbourne schools in the mornings. In the afternoons, equipped with safety pins and a copy or two of *Alice*, he went to the beach. He loved the sea, and there was always the chance of meeting a new child friend.

Late in the autumn he was in London to see J. M. Barrie's *Little Minister* at the Haymarket. A beautiful play, beautifully acted, he decided. A month later he sat up in his Christ Church study until four o'clock in the morning struggling with a mathematical poser sent him from New York. The point was to find three equal rational-sided

right-angle triangles. He found two but not the third.

He was ready packed, everything neatly done up in paper, the exact change in different compartments of his purse, to go home to Guildford the next day for the start of the Christmas vacation. He got there December 23 and went right to work on his *Symbolic Logic*. He was well and in good spirits.

On January 5, 1898, a telegram brought the unpleasant news that his brother-in-law, the Reverend C. S. Collingwood, father of Dodgson's biographer, had died. Dodgson planned to travel north to Sunderland in Durham the next day, but he awoke with a slight hoarseness and what seemed the beginnings of a cold. The family physician ordered him to bed when bronchial symptoms developed into influenza. A nurse was brought in.

Dodgson breathed with difficulty. He knew that he was very ill. "Take away those pillows. I shall need them no more," Collingwood reports his saying to a sister. He asked that a favorite hymn be read to him.

The Reverend Charles Lutwidge Dodgson died about half past two on the afternoon of January 14, 1898. He was within two weeks of his sixty-sixth birthday. Almost twenty-five years before, he had written exact "Directions Regarding My Funeral." He was buried in the simple fashion he had requested, in the Guildford cemetery.

On the marble cross later erected over his grave, the name Lewis Carroll was cut in parentheses under his own.

He loved the sea, and there was always the chance of meeting a new child friend.

Twelve

Eulogies were spoken and panegyrics were delivered when Charles Dodgson died. Oxford took solemn note of his passing, for he had spent forty-seven years of his life in Christ Church. The London newspapers carried obituaries and tributes, for of all his scores of publications two small books and some utterly nonsensical poems had made him one of England's literary figures. Men and women spoke out about his love for children, and children wrote of their love for him and his for them.

Yet here and there an odd note sounded. Not everybody had known him as a young man in white flannels and a straw boater, spilling golden words on a golden afternoon on the Isis to three enthralled small girls. Some had known him as a wit and raconteur at the high table in the Hall or in the senior Common Room, his stammer enhancing a droll story, his sharp wit pinking into the talk, his humor overflowing; but others had known him only as a hypercritical don jealous of his academic prerogatives, satirical about college plans and activities.

The great and the near-great had posed for the enthusiastic and exacting photographer. Little girls had delighted in his stories, the toys he brought out for them in his rooms, the tunes he played backwards on his orguinette, the walks during which their gentle companion had regaled them with jokes and riddles. He had treated them with a tender affection which they had recognized as different, and wonderfully different, from the speech and action of parents and governesses and nurses. They loved the slender, stiffly upright figure with the jerky step and the gentle face they saw more clearly as he approached them in The Parks or on the Oxford walks.

Yet fellow mathematicians had winced at his unpleasant antagonism in controversy, publishers had had to deal with a difficult author, and artists with an impossible taskmaster. Some men and women knew his generosity, for out of the substantial income from his books Dodgson had dealt liberally with his family and friends. When someone in need asked for a loan of a hundred pounds, he had usually refused and made the sum a gift instead. He saw to it that copies of his books were made freely available in children's hospitals. He paid for the music and acting lessons of small girls with stage ambitions and made certain that they met managers and actors with influence in the theatrical world.

Others had seen only the rather priggish parson in black broadcloth, tall hat, gray gloves, who insisted on rigid reverence, on the strict observance of the Sabbath; and still others only the whimsical eccentric who sent letters addressed to Lewis Carroll to the dead-letter office, used squares cut out of cardboard for place mats at his dinners to save the expense of linen, and turned brusquely away if anyone mentioned the *Alice* books.

He had been a delightful person when it pleased him to be delightful. He had not been as delightful in the lecture room or as curator of the Common Room. The indefatigable celebrity hunter and undiscourageable collector of autographs, who had affronted Prince Albert through his persistence, had been peremptory and unpleasant in his refusals when admirers asked for photographs or autographs of Lewis Carroll.

On the Sunday after Dodgson's death his friend Dean Paget spoke glowingly in Christ Church chapel of his gifts, his genius, his sense of humor, his simplicity, his "real and touching childlikeness." He paid tribute to Dodgson's brilliant and venturesome imagination, but he also acknowledged that men might differ "according to our difference of taste or temperament, in appraising Charles Dodgson's genius." He admitted, as if he were forced to, that there was "a certain disproportion, now and then, in the view he took of things."

Men had smarted under Dodgson's sarcasm, been bored by his solemn piety and occasionally insulted by his refusal of invitations he did not think it worth his while to accept. The Dodgson they knew, excitable, argumentative, disdainful of duller opponents, and often maddeningly pedantic, was not without conceit. These same men were amazed and must sometimes have been dismayed by the poetry, the lyric and satiric fancy, and the contagious nonsense of Lewis Carroll.

170

These were the men and women who had known the man. The hundreds of thousands, then the millions, of readers of the two *Alice* books, the *Snark*, and the *Sylvie and Bruno* books knew only Lewis Carroll. Children thought of him as theirs. It was a girl of fourteen who proposed, soon after Dodgson's death, in a letter to the *St. James Gazette* that children give money to establish a memorial cot in the Children's Hospital which would be called the Alice in Wonderland Cot. Money poured in from children, from public figures, and from friends. One of these was the Reverend Robinson Duckworth, who sent two pounds, two shillings, and a letter telling how he had been the Duck on the July 4, 1862 voyage up the Isis.

Years later, with Lewis Carroll's world fame secure, *The Times* of London launched a campaign that resulted in a larger memorial to Lewis Carroll, an entire children's ward in St. Mary's Hospital in Paddington. It was opened in November 1937.

On May 7, 1959, the bronze Alice in Wonderland Statue, a memorial to Margita Delacorte, was unveiled in Central Park in New York. The group by Jose de Kreeft stands at the north end of the Sailboat Lake above Seventy-second Street off Fifth Avenue. Alice sits on a giant mushroom, her kitten on her lap. The March Hare is before her to her right, the Mad Hatter to her left. The Dormouse is on a smaller mushroom. The Cheshire Cat looks over her shoulder. The Caterpillar is there, and the Lizard. On a fair day, small children are usually climbing up, under, and around the group. Alice and her friends are there for them. Cut into small stone slabs set in the ground around the statue are songs and verses from *Alice*: Twinkle, twinkle, little bat . . . Beautiful Soup . . . Speak roughly to your little boy

171

. . . Tweedledum and Tweedledee . . . They told me you had been to her . . . 'Twas brillig and the slithy toves . . .

Stuart Dodgson Collingwood warned in 1899, only a year after his uncle's death, against any unnatural division between the Reverend C. L. Dodgson and Lewis Carroll. Collingwood felt, in his words, that a real unity underlay both his life and all his writing. In 1954, Derek Hudson urged the same point. Yet the popular view persists because its appeal is almost irresistible. The contrast between the man Dodgson and the writer Carroll is too dramatic. Here, see this shy recluse of a mathematician who wrote *Alice in Wonderland!* It is incredible that such a man could have written such a book!

Charles Dodgson was never shy, and he was seldom a recluse. He was aloof only when, for reasons of his own, he wished to be. If he had not been Charles Lutwidge Dodgson, he could never have been Lewis Carroll. Given his ancestry, his boyhood background, his temperament, and the way in which he spent his life, it was not at all impossible that Charles Dodgson should write the *Alice* books and make them the books they are. It was almost inevitable.

Dodgson himself was largely responsible for the seeming dichotomy, the cutting in two. He insisted that he was Charles Lutwidge Dodgson, Student of Christ Church and Deacon of the Church of England, and that Lewis Carroll was an alien. He wrote and, when it pleased him, spoke as Lewis Carroll, but he was adamant about retaining his identity as the Reverend C. L. Dodgson.

The accident of his having used a pen name perpetuated the distinction between the two personalities. If Oliver Wendell Holmes had used a pen name, he might also have been viewed as a dual personality. He was a doctor of medicine and a professor in the Harvard Medical School at the same time that he was a novelist and a comic poet. Robert Bridges was a doctor. So was Somerset Maugham. Like Dodgson, Dean Swift was a churchman. All of these men used their own names in their professions and on their writings. Kenneth Grahame signed the same name as Secretary of the Bank of England and as author of *The Wind in the Willows*. Because Dodgson used a different name and denied the very existence of his *alter ego*, he has been regarded as a man incredibly divided by violently contrasting and even inimical personalities.

Dodgson was of the academic and clerical aristocracy. He was expected to excel in the university and in the Church. When he first published *Alice in Wonderland* he could not know whether the book would succeed, and he would not have wished a failure tagged to his name. By the time its success was established, Lewis Carroll was established too.

Certainly there were contradictions in Dodgson's character. There were disparate elements in him. It seems sometimes as if he were sharply and uncomfortably aware of them. Yet it is usual, not unusual, for there to be diverse elements in an individual; and the richer and more gifted the individual, the more and more sharply contrasting the expression of these diversities and contradictions is apt to be.

In actuality, Charles Dodgson was a closely integrated man of many talents who sought to express all that he was through many means: through his sketching pencil, his pen and typewriter, the theater, his religiousness, his delight in words, and above all through his love. It was love he celebrated in *Sylvie and Bruno*, where he named it love, and the love he felt for small girls that, underneath all the puns

173

and parodies, the satire, and the delectable nonsense, he expressed in *Alice's Adventures in Wonderland* and in *Through the Looking-Glass and What Alice Found There*.

The basic impulse for these books came out of emotions so deep within him that he was never able to explain the where or whence or how of the writing. He knew how he wrote his mathematical treatises and concocted his games. He knew how he built his sermons. He used his mind, his training, and all the utilitarian intelligence he could draw on. He was convinced that the *Alice* books, the *Snark*, and his other purely Carrollian writing came through sheer inspiration. He could never explain, even to himself.

Once when a small girl praised him for *Alice in Wonderland*, he chided her. "Never praise me. I feel myself a trustee, that is all."

He was talking of the Alice books when in 1887 he wrote:

> . . . every such idea and nearly every word of the dialogue, *came of itself*. Sometimes an idea comes at night, when I have had to get up and strike a light to note it down — sometimes when out on a lonely winter walk, when I have had to stop, and with half-frozen fingers jot down a few words which should keep the new-born idea from perishing — but whenever or however it comes, *it comes of itself*. I cannot set invention going like a clock, by any voluntary winding up: nor do I believe that any *original* writing (and what other kind is worth preserving?) was ever so produced. If you sit down, unimpassioned and uninspired, and *tell* yourself to write for so many hours, you will merely produce (at least I am sure I should merely produce) some

of that article which fills, so far as I can judge, two-thirds of most magazines — most easy to write, most weary to read . . . to my mind one of the most detestable things in modern literature. "Alice" and the "Looking-Glass" are made up almost wholly of bits and scraps, single ideas which came of themselves.

Notice how Dodgson almost helplessly keeps repeating the phrase "came of themselves." He could not explain. Notice also his *pride* that they did and his *scorn* of any other kind of writing. I italicize the two words because that is what he would have done.

The ideas and even fragments of dialogue for the *Sylvie and Bruno* stories came, as Dodgson said, "who knows how?" In his long preface to *Sylvie and Bruno* he says that they came to him

with a transitory suddenness that left me no choice but either to record them then and there, or to abandon them to oblivion. Sometimes one could trace to their source these random flashes of thought — as being suggested by the book one was reading, or struck out from the "flint" of one's own mind by the "steel" of a friend's chance remark — but they had also a way of their own, of occurring *à propos* of nothing — specimens of that hopelessly illogical phenomenon, "an effect without a cause."

He might not be able to explain it — it almost sounds as if he were glad he could not explain it — but Charles Dodgson took a high and justifiable pride in his artistry. Perhaps one reason he so often denied his identity as Lewis Carroll was that he hugged that identity and what he had accomplished through it jealously to himself and refused to share its preciousness with others who could not feel so deeply or begin to understand what it meant to him. He could trust this inner self only to small girls whom he loved and who, he hoped, loved him.

Ingenious and inventive, Charles Dodgson grew up on the lonely glebe farm in Daresbury. Instinctively he took it upon himself to entertain his five younger sisters. Rhyme came easily to him. So did reason. As Walter de la Mare remarked, there has seldom been a case where a boy was so clearly the father of the man he became.

Teaching mathematics at Christ Church was Dodgson's profession, his vocation. It came of his academic-clerical heritage and training imposed of a natural aptitude. Writing *Alice in Wonderland* and his other imaginative work sprang from temperamental necessity. It expressed his more insistent need. Charles Dodgson was no literary sport or Jekyll and Hyde phenomenon. He was at ease as don, photographer, theater-goer, logician, and imaginative writer. None of his careers was distortion.

Neither is it at all unusual that what are among the greatest children's books in the English language were written by a man who was unmarried and childless. Dean Swift never married. Edward Lear was a lifelong bachelor. Kate Greenaway never married. Beatrix Potter, whose delicate watercolors are as prized as her books about Peter Rabbit and all his friends, was childless.

A stickler about everything, Dodgson showed a formal exterior to his Oxford contemporaries. He shared his emotional life with small girls. Somewhere within himself was his real life. With his geometric neatness of mind he might have pictured this arrangement as three concentric circles. In the innermost and smallest circle of his reality was Lewis

176

Carroll. For all his logic, he may have been wrong about one thing. All his life he believed that Lewis Carroll was really Charles Lutwidge Dodgson. It may well be that the opposite was true, that Charles Dodgson was fundamentally Lewis Carroll.

The Charles Dodgson who told the fairy tale *Alice's Adventures Under Ground* on the Fourth of July 1862 was a young man, vital, eager, very much alive. The vital force remained strong in Dodgson, but it seemed to change direction and seek other expression as he grew older. He remained younger always than most men can in his sympathy with childhood, but in other ways he seemed to grow older faster, to lose the *élan* which must have characterized him that afternoon when the sun shone so brightly on the Isis.

Dodgson definitely changed in his late forties when, at almost the same time, he forswore both the photography of which he had been so impassioned an addict and so successful a practitioner, and his lectureship. He seemed to grow more subdued and repressed as he retreated into the intensity of his study of logic and mathematics. There may have been rebuffs and disappointments. There may have been external reasons for what seems like his partial withdrawal from life. Perhaps, and more likely, there were no definable reasons at all.

By his own choice or the dictates of temperament, he had kept himself at a little distance from life. Unfortunately and in the end, a man pays for assuming and maintaining the spectator attitude. He lives without taking part in ordinary life. The elasticity goes. The fastidious man becomes somewhat the fantastic man as the eccentricities developed in loneliness become more marked. Dodgson was so refined and delicate that he became rather attentuated. He lacked real life experience and probably, if not too consciously, was aware of it. His hypersensitiveness increased as his critical intelligence took further precedence over his creative impulse. He came into little contact with the stronger departments of life and human nature, and grew dessicated because he fed on meager food.

The insulation of Dodgson's life shows in his character and in his writing. His exquisiteness is the exquisiteness of the genteel, not the exquisiteness which some artists can distill from a fuller experience. Dodgson imagined his stories out of an experience which was literary, scientific, academic. The realities of his life were the realities of childhood, not those of mature life of which he knew little. He could not make up a believable plot, even when he tried, as in the adult frame of *Sylvie and Bruno*. He did not know life that well. He could do fantasy out of inventiveness in the safe realm of childhood.

All this is a matter of proportion. Dodgson was insulated and apart in Christ Church, but he was not isolated. A strongly marked character, he was very much part of his own tight little world and a courageous figure within it. It took courage for a don to flaunt the university authorities, as he often did. It took courage for a Victorian clergyman, whose own bishop had spoken out against it, to make the theater a vivid part of his life. It took courage for him to defy the conventions of the time in his association with small girls.

It was to one of them he wrote on New Year's Day of 1895:

You are quite correct in saying it is a long time since you have heard from me: in fact, I find that I

178

have not written to you since the 13th of last November. But what of that? You have access to the daily papers. Surely you can find out negatively, that I am all right! Go carefully through the list of bankruptcies; then run your eye down the police cases; and if you fail to find my name anywhere, you can say to your mother in a tone of calm satisfaction, "Mr. Dodgson is going on *well*."

It is pleasant to be able to report (in a tone of calm satisfaction) that Mr. Dodgson, Alice, the Duchess, the mad gardener, the Jabberwock, the White Knight, and the Snark — which was really a Boojum — still go on very well indeed.

CHARLES LUTWIDGE DODGSON

(Lewis Carroll)

1832 — January 27, born in Daresbury, Cheshire.

1843 — Family moved to Croft, Yorkshire.

1844 — Entered Richmond School.

1846 — Entered Rugby.

1850 — Matriculated at Christ Church, Oxford, May 23.

1851 — Entered Christ Church, January 24.

1852 — Made Student of Christ Church.

First Class Honors in Mathematics, head of list, October.

1854 — Received B.A. degree, December 18.

1856 — Appointed mathematical lecturer, Christ Church, in March.

Used name Lewis Carroll for first time in magazine *The Train.*

Ordered camera and photographic equipment, March 17.

Took first successful pictures, June 3.

1857 — Received Master of Arts degree.

1861 — Ordained as deacon in Church of England.

1862 — Told story of Alice's adventures to Edith, Alice, and Lorina Liddell on river excursion up the Isis to Godstow, July 4.

Began lettering and illustrating manuscript copy of the story, November 13.

1864 — Gave manuscript copy of *Alice's Adventures Under Ground* to Alice Liddell, Saturday, November 26.

1865 — *Alice's Adventures in Wonderland* published June 27.

Book reprinted in November.

1866 — First printing of *Alice* published in the United States.

1867 — Toured on Continent and in Russia with Reverend Henry Liddon, July 12 to September 13.

1868 — Archdeacon Dodgson, father, died in June. Sisters established family home in Guildford, Surrey.

1869 — *Phantasmagoria and Other Poems* published.

1871 — *Through the Looking-Glass and What Alice Found There* published December 6.

1876 — *The Hunting of the Snark* published in March.

1880 — Abandoned photography.

1881 — Resigned mathematical lectureship, last lecture November 30.

1882 — Became Curator, Christ Church Common Room.

1886 — Facsimile edition of *Alice's Adventures Under Ground* published.

1887 — *The Game of Logic* published.

1889 — *Sylvie and Bruno* published.

1893 — *Sylvie and Bruno Concluded* published.

1896 — *Symbolic Logic, Part I*, published.

1898 — Died in Guildford, January 14.

BIBLIOGRAPHY

Bede, Cuthbert, M. A. (Edward Bradley). *The Adventures of Mr. Verdant Green*. London: James Blackwood & Co., 1858.

Collingwood, Stuart Dodgson. *The Life and Letters of Lewis Carroll (Rev. C. L. Dodgson)*. New York: The Century Company, 1899.

Davidson, Angus. *Edward Lear, Landscape Painter and Nonsense Poet (1812–1888)*. New York: E. P. Dutton & Co., Inc., 1939.

De la Mare, Walter. *Lewis Carroll*. London: Faber & Faber, Ltd., 1932.

Dodgson, Charles Lutwidge. *Alice's Adventures Under Ground*. Being a facsimile of the original ms. book afterwards developed into "Alice's Adventures in Wonderland." New York: The Macmillan Company, 1932.

———. *Collected Verse of Lewis Carroll*. New York: The Macmillan Company, 1933.

———. *The Complete Works of Lewis Carroll*. New York: The Modern Library, 1936.

———. *Symbolic Logic* and *The Game of Logic*. New York: Dover Publications, Inc., 1958.

Gardner, Martin, ed. *The Annotated Alice*. New York: Clarkson N. Potter, Inc., 1960.

——. *The Annotated Snark*. New York: Simon and Schuster, Inc., 1962.

Gernsheim, Helmut. *Lewis Carroll, Photographer*. New York: Chanticleer Press, 1949.

Green, Roger Lancelyn, ed. *The Diaries of Lewis Carroll*. 2 vols. New York: Oxford University Press, 1954.

Hatch, Evelyn M., ed. *A Selection from the Letters of Lewis Carroll (The Rev. Charles Lutwidge Dodgson) to his Child-Friends*. London: Macmillan & Co., Ltd., 1933.

Hudson, Derek. *Lewis Carroll*. New York: The Macmillan Company, 1954.

Hutton, Laurence. *Literary Landmarks of Oxford*. New York: Charles Scribner's Sons, 1903.

Lear, Edward. *Nonsense Omnibus*. Intro. by Sir E. Strachey, Bart. London: Frederick Warne & Co., Ltd., 1943.

Lennon, Florence Becker. *Victoria Through the Looking-Glass: The Life of Lewis Carroll*. New York: Simon and Schuster, Inc., 1945.

Long, John E., "Oxford, Mother of Anglo-Saxon Learning," *The National Geographic Magazine*, November, 1929.

McDermott, John Francis, ed. *The Russian Journal and Other Selections from the Works of Lewis Carroll*. New York: E. P. Dutton & Co., Inc., 1935.

Madan, Falconer. *The Lewis Carroll Centenary in London, 1932*. London: Messrs. J. & E. Bumpus, Ltd., 1932.

Moses, Belle. *Lewis Carroll in Wonderland and at Home*. New York and London: D. Appleton & Co., 1910.

Taylor, Alexander L., M.A. *The White Knight, A Study of C. L. Dodgson (Lewis Carroll)*. Edinburgh: Oliver & Boyd, 1952.

184